REPORT WRITING
———— FOR ————
INTERNAL AUDITORS

D1297002

ANGELA J. MANIAK

BANKERS PUBLISHING COMPANY
PROBUS PUBLISHING COMPANY
Chicago, Illinois
Cambridge, England

A Bankline Publication

ISBN 1-55520-132-6

Printed in the United States of America

4 5 6 7 8 9 0

Contents

Preface

Reporting audit results to management is the most important and demanding part of your job as an internal auditor. The value of your work comes not from the gathering of information, but from your assessment and presentation of it. Management's awareness and acceptance of your conclusions and its prompt action in response to reported problems are your measures of success.

This book will help you write audit reports that get the attention of your readers, build acceptance, and encourage action. It provides you with guidelines, techniques, and examples to help you choose the appropriate substance, organization, tone, and style of each report you write.

New staff auditors as well as experienced audit managers will benefit from the book's principles. Writers and reviewers will learn specific standards for audit report writing, identify the criteria that must be met consistently, and understand the variable factors that influence the tone and substance of audit reports. They will learn to apply these concepts in their own writing and editing. They will also be able to share their understanding of these concepts so that they can write and distribute reports more promptly.

Because this book progresses through each logical step in writing and reviewing an audit report, you may use it according to your own needs. New auditors should read through the book beginning to end to understand fully the principles of audit reporting. Struggling writers will find particular sections of the book a useful reference as they compose. Managers can review relevant chapters to evaluate the quality of their department's reports and learn how to give constructive feedback to writers.

The Introduction includes two chapters that set the framework for audit report writing. Chapter 1 identifies the quality and cost components of audit reports and asks you to analyze your own reporting. Chapter 2 helps writers apply a disciplined logic for developing the content of their reports.

"Writing to Inform" provides guidelines to help you select and present just the right amount of information to executive management. The two chapters help you get and keep your readers' attention.

"Writing to Persuade" helps you develop the ability to convince your audience to accept your recommendations and take quick, practical action. This section considers the resistance your audience may offer to your reports and equips you to overcome objections.

"Presenting to Senior Management" offers techniques for effective written and oral presentations to senior management and the audit committee.

"Using Effective Style" enables you to choose a style appropriate to your topic and audience and to write in readable, inviting language.

Finally, "Editing and Reviewing" outlines principles for effective self-review and constructive editing of others' writing.

This book's objective is to help you solve the report-writing problems you face on your job. It is not designed as a quick fix, offering tips on grammar or confining itself to measurements of readability. It emphasizes the fundamental difficulties of composing audit reports: how to present negative issues constructively, how to write a balanced report, how to select the appropriate amount of information to report to senior management. These challenges are unique to audit reports. As a result, the book presents examples and developed techniques that are unique to audit report writing. General principles of organization and readability offer limited help to the auditor. The audit-specific guidance provided here offers practical solutions.

These principles and techniques were developed in response to auditors' requests for easy-to-use, effective writing tools. The checklists, worksheets, and decision-making tools offered in this book have been used extensively in workshops and on the job. I share them here with confidence that you will make the same practical use of these guidelines.

Acknowledgment

My clients, workshop participants, and colleagues have all influenced the ideas that appear in this book by raising practical challenges, questioning the completeness of my guidance, and sharing samples of their writing. I am indebted to each one of them for their contributions.

INTRODUCTION

1

The Value of the Internal Audit Report

Each audit report you produce is likely to cost your organization between $10,000 and $100,000. How do you measure what management is getting in return for that price? What steps do you take to make sure each report fits senior management's needs? What quality-control steps do you have in place to guarantee that you are producing the best report possible? If you do not have answers to these questions, you may be overlooking or shortchanging one of your most powerful tools—the internal audit report.

The audit report plays a unique and influential role in your organization. It is one of a handful of documents distributed regularly to senior management, the Board of Directors, and the Audit Committee. The audit report includes recommendations for changes in procedures and standards; it calls attention to high-risk areas; it reports your evaluation of the quality of systems and procedures. On the basis of these reports, management decides on directions, strategies, and priorities. Acceptance of audit recommendations may influence the costs and the profits of your organization.

It is these reports your management pays for when funding internal auditing. In senior management's eyes, these documents are the only products you produce. Plans, budgets, workpapers, and risk assessments are all tools you use to build that final product.

In the internal auditor's eyes, though, reports may be of more bother than value. The bulk of audit time is budgeted for planning and fieldwork. Audit managers focus their review and evaluation of work on these parts of the job. The report may seem a nuisance, consuming too much of the audit group's time to write, edit, and issue.

The fact is that report writing is difficult and does require a great deal of time. Your job is to produce the highest quality report possible while controlling the cost of its production. The goal of this book is to help you do that job well—to enable you to write reports that command senior management's attention, show the value of internal audit's contribution to the organization, and are deemed worthy of every dollar they cost.

What Are the Purposes of the Audit Report?

Internal audit reports serve the purposes of management, not of auditors. Therefore, to produce a quality report, you must first determine how management will use your report. As executives direct and monitor the organization, they look to internal auditing to keep them aware of current risks, problem areas, and control issues. If problems or risks are identified in an audit report, management wants to know what action is being or has been taken to resolve them. In deciding whether or not to act on audit recommendations, managers need to accept the validity and significance of the audit points. The business purposes of the audit report, then, are to:

- Inform,
- Persuade, and
- Get results.

Inform. Executive readers want to be made aware of the results of your work and kept informed of your conclusions. Your report must present these key points in a style that is easy and quick for management to comprehend.

Persuade. Information presented to senior-level management must be of direct significance to the organization. Line management must be convinced of the benefits of recommendations before it will agree to act; senior management must see the value of information presented before it will lend support to internal auditing.

Get results. The ultimate value of an audit report is its ability to promote action. The acceptance of recommended changes for reducing risk, preventing problems, and correcting errors is the expected result of a report. All auditing and all reporting methods lead to this key purpose: getting results.

Audit reports are not written to describe the amount of auditing done, to document operating procedures, or to educate readers about the details of systems and policies. Attempting to meet these goals in your reports will cloud their focus, decrease their hold on the readers' attention, and weaken their persuasive force. Audit reports present your department's conclusions and recommendations. If your management calls on you to meet some of the other goals described here, do so in other types of documents. Do not compromise the objectives of internal audit reporting by trying to accomplish goals other than those leading to action on audit recommendations.

Quality Standards for Internal Audit Reports

Writing effectively for your high-level audience requires you to understand expectations and define quality standards that can meet those expectations. You must solicit reactions and comments from senior management to find out how well your reports are meeting needs. You must be responsive to management's particular requests for content, style, or frequency of your reporting. While each organization's key managers will have specific needs, certain standards are consistently demanded by executive readers. The list of eight quality standards presented below summarizes the characteristics your readers look for in your reports.

Executive management expects your reports to be:

Direct. Readers expect a straightforward and factual presentation of results. Cushioning, qualifying, or burying key findings exasperates readers who are looking for conclusions and recommendations. Direct reports inform readers quickly, using:

- Conclusive opening sentences,
- Informative headings, and
- Presentation of main points first.

Succinct. Brief statements, capsulizing key ideas, say more than long explanations that detail all components of a thought. Busy

3

readers demand compact presentations. Quality, compact reports result from:

- Limited detail,
- Selection of items of greatest significance,
- Summaries of supporting data, and
- Concise style.

Appropriate. Each report must use a tone and strategy appropriate to the significance of information presented. Report language should be creative; word choice and organization should reflect the varying degrees of significance among items presented. Reports are most appropriate when writers remember to:

- Know the readers' interests,
- Select the proper emphasis, and
- Present relevant and valid information.

Persuasive. Readers need to care about the information you present before they are motivated to act on it. Audit reports must be relevant to the business, describing risks of findings and benefits of recommendations. Persuasive reports include:

- Convincing support for conclusions,
- Effects of conditions described, and
- Quantification of their impact.

Constructive. Critical reporting elicits antagonism, not cooperation. Content and language should be selected to show positive benefits and gain commitment from readers. Constructive reports present:

- Causes, not symptoms, of problems,
- Balance of positive and negative, and
- Credit for management action.

Results-oriented. Executives are not reading simply to find out about problems, but rather to learn about solutions. Effective reports emphasize results by including:

- Measurable and specific recommendations,
- Practical, action-oriented solutions, and
- Description of management action taken.

Inviting. Your report will get more attention if it is inviting to read, not intimidating. Reports that attract readers are those that include:

- Executive summaries,
- A professional format, and
- Brief, clearly labeled sections.

Timely. The value of audit reports is directly related to the speed with which the information is acted upon. Auditors keep their information timely by using:

- Immediate presentation to line management,
- Interim reports for serious issues, and
- Strict enforcement of standards of timeliness.

Cost Components of Internal Audit Reports

As you develop and meet the quality goals outlined above, you must also control the cost of achieving the standards. Only then can you create the greatest value, balancing the investment with the payback.

Analytical Costs

The time required to complete the audit itself, including planning, fieldwork, and development and presentation of conclusions, is the largest cost component of the report. The number of audit days times the average daily staff cost determines the cost for producing the substance of the report.

Administrative Costs

Additional cost comes from the administrative time required to issue reports, including time spent on the development of reporting standards, the definition of formats, and the training and instruction provided to staff. These costs are absorbed in chunks, rather than consumed at the time of each audit.

For each audit, additional time is needed to complete production, including composing the report, management review and editing, and typing, proofreading, and copying.

Agreement Costs

The report's value is not achieved until you have reached agreement with management and issues have been resolved. The time it takes to present the report, agree on solutions, and follow-up on any unresolved items after the report is issued are components of the cost of agreement.

Achieving quality standards while controlling cost will enable you to better measure the value of your reports and identify the payback management receives from investment in your work. Direct, persuasive, results-oriented reports benefit all levels of management, by keeping them informed, building their acceptance, and leading to positive change.

Balancing the Cost and Quality of Reporting

Value = Quality - Cost
Goal   Keep quality ratings high.
           Control costs, especially administrative.

Cost Components	**Quality Components**
Analytical: Planning & Fieldwork	Directness Succinctness

Administrative:
    Composing, Reviewing
    & Editing, Typing &
    Proofreading
	Appropriateness
	
	Persuasiveness
	
	Constructive Tone

Agreement:
    Presentation, Solution &
    Follow-Up
	Orientation Toward Results
	Inviting Look and Sound
	Timeliness

2

Getting Started: Writing the First Draft

The standards of quality and timeliness are not as easily attained as they are defined. If your reports are issued later than you would like, or if your report drafts are not of the highest quality and require a great deal of time to review and edit, you are not alone. Many audit departments share the goal of reducing the time it takes to produce reports while increasing the quality of drafts. At one time or another, every auditor has worked to meet this challenge.

You can find solutions to this challenge, for the timeliness and quality of your final report are a direct result of the process you use for writing. How and when you compose the draft, organize research data, and begin the review of the draft report by line and audit management influence your ability to write the highest quality report in the shortest amount of time.

Scheduling Writing Time

Audit staff and management complain that time is the biggest obstacle for most auditors writing reports. Staff members argue that there is not enough time for report writing, and managers argue that too much time is spent writing and reviewing reports. These conflicting views will remain a fact for most audit departments. There is no procedure that will create more time for report writing at the end of the audit. You may allocate, or simply take, more time to finish the report, but you will be subtracting those hours from the budget for other work; something else will suffer while you take additional days to write. Likewise, whatever amount of time you use to compose and issue reports may be perceived as too much, since the cost of your audit will increase as you put more time into the report. This fact alone may motivate you to shorten the writing schedule. Your likely preference for auditing over writing will help you set your priorities—more time auditing to arrive at results, less time writing and editing to get those results published.

Time dedicated to writing is not as precisely measurable as that spent on other parts of the audit process. Nevertheless, it is usually scheduled in modular segments, the same as planning, fieldwork, and testing. A chunk of time is set up for report writing after the completion of fieldwork, and the report draft is scheduled to be issued within a certain time frame. During those days, auditors are expected to sit down and write the report, and managers are expected to review, edit, and approve the draft.

This logical scheduling of writing seldom seems to work in the way it is planned. By the time auditors complete their fieldwork and return to their desks to start writing, they are likely to be behind schedule. Perhaps the five days they had allocated for wrapping up the audit have been reduced to one. If there has been a change in scope or extension of the fieldwork, the allocation for report writing may have disappeared completely. These time constraints not only mean that auditors are rushed to complete the report, but also that other demands are being made on these same auditors' time. The next scheduled audit is already being planned, and their attention is required for that. Administrative odds and ends need to be handled while the auditors are available in the office for a few days. These competing demands distract the writer, and he or she may not give full attention to the report. With these pressures, auditors become eager to get the writing out of the way. To appease their manager, who keeps asking when the report will be done, they take an afternoon, compose a draft, and turn it in for review, hoping that the boss won't send it back with too many changes or suggested revisions.

Procrastination and Perfectionism

Even when the obstacle of limited time is removed, writers may not score much better in efficiency. "I don't know where to start" is a common explanation for delays. "There is so much data from this audit, I am not sure yet how I am going to organize the report." Other auditors also cite uncertainty: not knowing what their boss wants. "My bosses seem to change their minds about what they want from one report to another. I want to see how they edit one report before I start another." Some auditors delay their writing because they are not confident of their own abilities. "I'm likely to write a draft that's not very good and then have to rewrite it. I'd rather wait until I know exactly what I am going to say, and then compose the report." These explanations are representative of the barriers many auditors face when writing. Most of the rationalizing points to two causes of their writer's block: procrastination and perfectionism.

Procrastination is a self-imposed delay. Not knowing where to start, having other things to do, not being able to schedule time with the boss—these are all excuses for not sitting down and writing. Writing may be one of the difficult and time-consuming parts of the job, complicated by editorial feedback that is more often critical than complimentary. These negative expectations cause auditors to procrastinate. It is more rewarding to do the easier things, and so they do those first and put off report writing until the last possible moment.

Perfectionism prevents writers from getting started because they are afraid of making mistakes or because they insist on writing the report from start to finish without revision. They are likely to describe their delays in these terms: "I don't know yet what my opening line is going to be. Once that comes to me, I'll be able to get started and write the rest of the report." Or: "It feels as if it takes forever to write one page. The process is so slow, it's discouraging."

The result of both tendencies—procrastination and perfectionism—is an even tighter restriction of the time available for report writing. By putting off the task, writers end up in a greater time crunch. When they do compose the draft, they have little time to revise and fine tune their writing. They are likely to turn in their report draft feeling unsure of its quality, and when reviewers receive the draft, they catch the mistakes that have slipped by the writer: the unclear word, the imprecise data, the grammatical error. While the auditors have not had enough time to write a quality report, the managers are now taking too much time reviewing and correcting the draft.

Breaking out of this syndrome requires a change in thinking as well as in the process of writing. Composition of a narrative does not begin at the moment you complete the fieldwork, and it does not flow from introduction, to the first and most important audit comment, and sequentially through the remaining comments and recommendations. The final product is linear, brief, and smooth-flowing, but the process of getting there is circular, time-consuming, and choppy. As you write, you clarify your thinking. Finding the right words to put on paper requires you to refine your reasoning, to know exactly what message you want to convey to your readers. The writer's common lament, "I don't know what I want to say," is legitimate. As you begin to put ideas on paper, however, they become clearer. You reason through the detailed information, draw connections between stray thoughts and isolated pieces of data, and form tentative conclusions about the information. You experiment with different ways of organizing information and try different words to get across just the right emphasis and tone. It may take several versions before you create the draft that says just the right thing.

Forcing yourself to sit down and write a report logically from beginning to end goes against this natural thinking process, and it causes the frustration and dissatisfaction so many auditors experience when writing. To resolve the conflict, you must recognize and accept that composition may be difficult. You must allow yourself to make false starts and write imperfect sentences. You must free yourself from the constraints of a report structure and let yourself begin writing anywhere within the report, without concern for what comes first, second, and last.

You must also schedule your writing to accommodate this circular process. To allow time for ideas to form, you need to begin getting ideas on paper early in the audit process. To compose efficiently at the end of the audit, you have to begin thinking about the report from the start. Summarizing, drawing tentative conclusions, and writing outlines along the way will help you complete the first steps of report writing even before you finish fieldwork. These techniques will allow you to start composing the report with a stack of outlines and narratives already in hand, and they will help you concentrate your time after fieldwork on refining your thoughts, polishing your language, and producing the best report possible.

Composing a high-quality, timely report draft requires ongoing planning and summarizing throughout fieldwork and the use of time-saving techniques as you compose. Following these principles can help you overcome delays and barriers in producing your reports:

- Write along the way.

- Use standard components and frameworks to structure your thoughts.

- Check for agreement on substance and strategy.
- Compose the full report quickly and polish the final product.

Write Along the Way

So much of the fieldwork is spent documenting work that you may think "writing along the way" is a natural product of your testing. Everything you do results in a workpaper. But if you have ever tried to use sections of your workpapers directly in an audit report you have probably found that the workpaper structure is quite different from that of reports. A typical workpaper summary—outlining objective, summary of testing, and conclusion—is designed for ease of reviewing results of testing, not for incorporation into a report.

Without adding bulk or burden to your workpapers, you can build in a different kind of summary serving a dual purpose— documenting results and providing material for the report. This summary should be in narrative or outline form and should include elements relevant to a management report, not just to audit workpapers. These elements should include a conclusion about the data, your analysis of the meaning or significance of the data, your thoughts on how to present the conclusion persuasively, and your identification of the most important data emerging from the detailed testing. As you begin to write down your thoughts, you record your initial analysis, allowing you to see these ideas on paper and refine your thinking as the audit progresses.

This first writing step is one of generating ideas. In each section of your audit testing, allow a space at the end of your workpapers for recording report ideas. Write your thoughts on these pages as they occur to you, and remember to fill out these pages when you finish a section of audit work.

Blank pages or worksheets will work equally well. Two helpful worksheets are presented here as Exhibits 2-1 and 2-2. The first worksheet, Dumping Ideas, encourages you to record any ideas that occur to you in any order. This "dumping ground" will hold your ideas until you are ready to select the best ones, combine others, and discard less relevant information. The second, the Planning Worksheet, will help you organize your thoughts for report presentation. For any topic you are considering presenting, you should be able to answer the questions on that summary page.

EXHIBIT 2-1

Dumping Ideas

Topic or section:
_____

Key ideas:
_____
_____
_____
_____
_____
_____
_____
_____
_____
_____
_____
_____
_____
_____
_____
_____
_____
_____
_____
_____
_____
_____
_____
_____
_____

EXHIBIT 2-2

Planning Worksheet

Topic or section:

_____

_____

_____

_____

Conclusion or key message:

_____

_____

_____

_____

Key points supporting the conclusion:

_____

_____

_____

_____

Action I would like to see taken:

_____

_____

_____

_____

The impression I want to convey to the reader:

_____

_____

_____

_____

By incorporating these worksheets into every section of your workpapers, you will be able to record your ideas efficiently and consistently. The worksheets will require little time to complete, because you will be turning to these pages to record your ideas as they occur. They will be readily available when you begin composing the full report, and you will know exactly where to turn to find them. Stray notes, separate pages, or miscellaneous notes to yourself tend to get lost along the way. These worksheets are consistent and easy to hold onto.

Planning worksheets are especially effective tools. Even if you take 30 minutes to complete these pages after finishing a section of testing, you will save twice that amount of time when you are writing at the end of the audit. These worksheets require you to start putting your information into a reporting structure, to state your tentative conclusion about the data, and to start selecting the key pieces of information supporting that idea. You will also develop your initial ideas on the recommendation and the finding's significance. Exhibit 2-3 shows a completed Planning Worksheet.

Use Standard Components to Structure Your Thoughts

The Dumping and Planning Worksheets will be useful for any writing project you do. A standard audit, a special project, a research report, or a systems development audit can all be summarized along the way using these worksheets. Even though the final reports for such projects will have different formats, the general summary sheets will be relevant to each.

Since internal audits and other types of projects usually result in a standardized report structure, you can take advantage of this consistency and save time by using the known elements and organizational patterns as you document ideas during fieldwork. Versions of the planning worksheets tailored to your report criteria will help you write outlines you can use directly in your final product.

For most audit reports, the standard components are the elements of audit comments: condition, criteria, effect, cause, and recommendation. Organizing your thoughts around these elements will enable you to develop a logical conclusion and persuasive presentation to management. Thinking about audit results in these terms will help you make the transition from raw data to a management

EXHIBIT 2-3

Sample Completed Planning Worksheet

Topic or section:
Loan collateral

Conclusion or key message:
Loan collateral is not consistently documented.

Key points supporting the conclusion:
8 of 40 files tested (20%) did not have evidence of collateral.

Officers listed collateral, but documentation was not on file.

Value of missing collateral items was $800,000.

Action I would like to see taken:
Include a follow-up administrative step to secure documentation.

The impression I want to convey to the reader:
If these become problem loans, the bank may not be able to collect.

The amount of these loans is at risk.

report. This outline will help you focus your thoughts on the most important information, weed out extraneous data, consider the business significance of your results, and analyze the cause of problems identified. Completing an Audit Comment Worksheet for any item you are considering presenting to management will give you an outline you can use for your oral presentation as well as for your written report. A sample of the Audit Comment Worksheet is shown in Exhibit 2-4.

Although every audit comment may not include answers to all five questions on the worksheet, the analytical process remains the same for each item you present. If you cannot answer one of the questions immediately, skip over it. Ideas may develop as you complete other sections of work. If you conclude that one or more questions are not relevant, document that conclusion on the worksheet.[1]

Check for Agreement on Substance and Strategy

With the worksheets completed, you will have outlines of your conclusions and audit comments in hand by the time you finish fieldwork. Not only will you have substance for your report, you will also have a summary of your results ready to present to audit and line management. Review can begin immediately once the Audit Comment Worksheets are written.

Besides reviewing detailed workpapers as they are completed, audit supervisors should also evaluate the substance of the Comment Worksheets. This will ensure agreement on key points before they are presented orally to line management, and will speed up the review of the report draft later in the process. The supervisor can evaluate the strength of the data supporting the statement of condition and determine if that statement reflects the appropriate emphasis. This early review can also improve the brainstorming done on the more persuasive items, such as Effect and Recommendation.

Once the auditor and supervisor agree on these outlines, the outlines can be used as drafts for presentation to line management. Some auditors prefer to give management copies of these worksheets; others like to use them as outlines for their oral presentations.

---

[1] For a more detailed discussion of the five elements of audit comments, see Angela J. Maniak, *Writing Effective Audit Reports* (Altamomte Springs, FL: The Institute of Internal Audits, 1986), pp. 43-56.

EXHIBIT 2-4

Audit Comment Worksheet

CONDITION (What is the control weakness, problem, or exception?)
_____
_____
_____
_____

CRITERIA (What standard should be met?)
_____
_____
_____
_____

EFFECT (What are the business implications of the condition?)
_____
_____
_____
_____

CAUSE (Why did the situation occur?)
_____
_____
_____
_____

RECOMMENDATION
(What should be done to correct and prevent the problem?)
_____
_____
_____
_____

17

Compose the Full Report Quickly and Polish the Final Product

When you are done with fieldwork, the content of your report is already developed. Instead of facing that dreaded task of writing a full report, you only have to complete the final steps of composition—organizing the comments, consolidating related items, writing a summary and conclusion, editing for style and clarity, and formatting for a professional presentation.

This phase should now be completed quickly, taking one-half to one day to complete. To be sure you can accomplish this step efficiently, set aside uninterrupted time. Four straight hours of composing will take you a lot farther than four interrupted hours. Put aside administrative work, phone calls, and spur-of-the-moment meetings. If necessary, move to a location other than your desk, where you won't need to answer your phone and people won't come looking for you. Avoid any excuses to procrastinate at this point.

Your first step is to pull the Comment Worksheets from your workpapers and organize them. Put related items together and prioritize them. Consolidate items that are closely related: problems having a common cause, exceptions resulting from the same control weakness, or items having similar effects on the business.

Keep a pad of paper beside you as you organize these pages. New ideas, effective phrases, and exact word choices may occur to you as you are reviewing the worksheets. Record thoughts immediately and incorporate them at the appropriate points as you write the narrative.

Write a summary of your major results and a conclusion addressing the audit objectives. With all the pieces now composed, go back through the full report, editing for style, conciseness, and clarity. Finally, consider appropriate formatting, making sure there are enough headings to guide the reader, that the length of sections and paragraphs is inviting, and that each part of the report flows comfortably to the next.

Put the report draft aside. Allow enough time—preferably overnight—for you to return to review the report objectively. Read it again, looking for coherence, flow, clarity, and style. Now, just two to three days after completing fieldwork, the report is ready for audit management's review and final distribution.

Breaking out of writer's block and eliminating the delays resulting from it require discipline. You can build that discipline into the routine of auditing by writing along the way, using worksheets and summaries to document and review audit comments as you develop them. Incorporate report writing into the audit process, following these steps.

Phase One: Fieldwork

1. Write the objective and scope.

2. Use Dumping and Planning Worksheets to gather information.

3. Complete Audit Comment Worksheets.

4. Review the substance of audit comments, using the Worksheets.

5. Present outline of audit comments to line management.

6. Decide on overall organization of report.

Phase Two: Report Production

7. Write report draft, including summary and conclusion.

8. Edit for style, conciseness, and clarity.

9. Present final report to management.

Developing report outlines and narratives as you audit will enable you to issue timely reports to management. Reports can be issued days—not weeks—after fieldwork. Quality will remain high, with writers and managers having had several opportunities to clarify their thinking, change their emphasis, and choose the most persuasive supporting evidence.

WRITING TO INFORM

3

Getting Your
Readers' Attention

Your best chance to capture your readers' attention is in your first sentence. Busy executives are demanding of every piece of paper they pick up and impatient with documents that do not make their points quickly and directly. Senior managers want reports they can evaluate easily by skimming through, identifying the key message, and deciding if they want or need to read more. Your reports are in competition with other tasks for your readers' time. By making each opening sentence or paragraph compact, direct, and interesting, you can create reports that get attention, invite your audience to read more, and generate a positive, quick response from management. You do not want your readers to have to work at identifying your message.

William Zinsser, a noted author on the skill of writing, puts it this way:

> "The most important sentence in any article is the first one. If it doesn't induce the reader to proceed to the second sentence, your article is dead." [1]

Readers' demands for informative and interesting beginnings put the burden of clarity squarely on the writer's shoulders. Rather than allowing readers to make their own interpretations of information or requiring readers to decipher the meaning of words, a good writer makes the message absolutely clear. That clarity may require a good deal of work on the part of the writer. Jacques Barzun, in *Simple & Direct*, explains it this way:

---

[1] William Zinsser, *On Writing Well* (New York: Harper & Row, 1980); p. 59.

23

Few people organize their thoughts and words in fully intelligible remarks. It seems easier to use a sort of oral shorthand and rely on the listener to jump to the right conclusion. He often fails. You correct him or he asks questions to settle his uncertainty. With a written text there is no opportunity to ask questions. All the reader has is words and punctuation marks. It follows that these must be set right—right for the purpose and right for the reader. *Rhetoric is the craft of setting down words and marks right; or again:* Rhetoric shows you how to put words together so that the reader not simply may but must grasp your meaning.[2]

To write an effective, attention-getting opening and to make your message absolutely clear, these techniques are effective:

- State your conclusion directly.

- Write concretely and descriptively.

- Use terms your readers understand.

- Choose the information of greatest interest to your reader.

- Design your opening to guide the reader.

Examples of Openings

For a writer, meeting expectations for a strong opening may be a difficult task. Many writers tend to start by writing something that comes to mind easily, and an effective first sentence is seldom easy to write.

The following examples of audit comments illustrate several methods auditors commonly use to begin their narratives.

EXAMPLE 1
Reconciliation

Regulation 9, section 7.2, requires that the assets held in or for a fiduciary account be reviewed at least annually and within 15 months of the last review. Trust uses a manual

---

[2] Jacques Barzun, *Simple & Direct* (New York: Harper & Row, 1985); p.2.

control log to schedule and record annual asset review dates. The "Assets Under Management" report provides a listing of fiduciary accounts managed. No reconciliation of the manual control log to the "Assets Under Management" report was performed during the audit period. The unit was unable to ensure that all fiduciary accounts subject to Regulation 9 were properly reviewed. A reconciliation of the manual control log to the report would ascertain that all fiduciary accounts were included in the manual control log and subsequently scheduled for an annual asset review.

EXAMPLE 2
Regulation B

We tested for compliance with Regulation B by sampling thirty-five rejected applications, and selected fifty-five accepted applications. This sample size was to provide a 97% reliability that there is no more than a 3.0% error rate. In summary, the results of our tests noted the following:

1. On average, it took 39 days to notify applicants of rejection decisions. Six rejection letters were mailed to applicants in excess of 65 days after the rejection decisions.

2. Approximately 120 items dated January remained in the pending file as of March 1.

EXAMPLE 3
Operating Expenses

Procedures for reporting operating expenses should be improved. Our review of the statements for the last three months disclosed the following exceptions:

1. Maintenance and security expenses were overstated in each month, totaling $75,000.

2. Mailing expenses were overstated on the input sheet by $12,250.

EXAMPLE 4
Cash Disbursement

During our audit of cash disbursements, it was noted that in some instances merchandise invoices were not properly approved for payment. Thirty-six invoices were selected for testing, and it was determined that 14 were not properly approved by purchasing personnel.

Analysis of the Openings

The opening lines of these four comments represent opening styles frequently used by auditors. Let's examine their content and then determine how well they get the readers' attention.

Example	Content of Opening Sentence
1	Background/Explanation of procedures
2	Audit procedures followed
3	Cliche/Ambiguous language
4	Context/Conclusion

These openings are not particularly effective in drawing attention. Readers are interested in the results of your work—the conclusions, facts, or effects of the situations you have tested. They are less interested in what the unit does (background) and what you did to reach your conclusion (procedures). This information interests the reader only as it supports or clarifies the message you present. Neither are readers attracted by cliches. "Procedures... should be improved," the opening line from Example 3, could be used for any audit comment. It is predictable, vague, and weak in its informational power. "During our audit of cash disbursements, it was noted that..." states the obvious. The reader knows that your results were achieved "during the audit" and that you "noted" the items you are presenting.

Auditors have logical reasons for beginning their comments with background or procedural information. Their goal is to give the readers information that may be needed to make sense of the findings. To understand why lack of reconciliation of the control log is a problem, the auditor reasons, you must first know the Regulation

9 requirements the log is supposed to help fulfill. To be convinced that the number of exceptions presented in Example 2 is significant, you must know the size and reliability of the sample selected. This logic represents the research method used in most testing and research, including internal auditing, and follows this thought pattern: what I did, what I found, what my findings mean.

Audit report writing, however, requires a different pattern of logic—that of your readers. Their thought sequence is:

- What is your conclusion?

- What support do you have?

- Why is this important?

- What should we do?

State Your Conclusion Directly

To capture and hold your readers' attention, answer their questions in the order listed above. Begin each comment with the last step of your fieldwork—the conclusion. Remember to start at the bottom, as illustrated by the differences between your workpaper summary and your audit comment worksheet as shown in Exhibit 3-1.

An opening that describes results may consist of a conclusion, specific facts, or both. For example:

> "Commercial loan documentation is incomplete. Twenty-five percent of the 100 files reviewed were missing insurance documents, 18% were lacking collateral information, and 12% did not have all required signatures."

The first sentence draws a broad conclusion. The second offers supporting evidence. A writer wanting to focus more on the facts and less on the overall conclusion might delete the first sentence and present only the statistics. On the other hand, the writer beginning with "Commercial loan documentation is incomplete" cannot stop there. This generalization needs the support of the statistics that follow.

This example avoids references to audit procedures, yet incorporates references to scope and sample size into the statement of results. Instead of saying, "We reviewed 100 loan files and noted that 25 of them were missing insurance documents," the writer summarizes this data into "25% of the 100 files reviewed." The examples presented at

EXHIBIT 3-1

Audit Workpaper Summary

Objective

Scope of Work

Results of Testing

Conclusion

Audit Comment Worksheet

Condition

Criteria

Effect

Cause

Recommendation

the start of this chapter could be revised to follow this format. In Example 2, the auditor might summarize the results: "Of 35 rejected applications tested, six letters were mailed more than 65 days after the credit decision was made." The references to the reliability of the statistical sample can be eliminated. The report is not the vehicle for justifying sampling or other testing techniques. If you have presented this orally to line management, you may not need it in the report at all. If senior management does like to see this information, it could be put in an appendix describing detailed testing.

Example 4 can be summarized in a similar way. A revision might read: "Fourteen of 36 invoices tested were not properly approved by purchasing personnel."

Limit the amount of background information and procedural description you give your readers, also. To determine what information you need, ask these questions:

- Will the reader understand the terms used?

- What explanation does the reader need?

- How much information does the reader want?

Consider your audience. Line management already knows the background you are presenting. Senior management may not know the detail, but may not be interested in a step-by-step description of operations or regulatory requirements. If it is senior management's needs you are addressing in providing background, you must present it carefully and concisely.

Let's go back to Example 1. The first three sentences give background. How much of this is needed?

Regulation 9, section 7.2, requires that the assets held in or for a fiduciary account be reviewed at least annually and within 15 months of the last review. Trust uses a manual control log to schedule and record annual asset review dates. The "Assets Under Management" report provides a listing of fiduciary accounts managed.

The underscored items below represent the information that may be both unknown and important to senior management.

Regulation 9, section 7.2, requires that the assets held in or for a *fiduciary account* be *reviewed at least annually* and within 15 months of the last review. Trust uses a manual control log to schedule and record annual asset review dates. The "Assets Under Management" report provides a listing of fiduciary accounts managed.

Now let's see how we can weave this information into a more direct opening line. The statement of conclusion in the original version is: "The unit was unable to ensure that all fiduciary accounts subject to Regulation 9 were properly reviewed." This includes the needed reference to Regulation 9, but does not define what "properly reviewed" means. A clear and direct opening sentence that more precisely describes proper review might be : "The unit does not have a reconciliation procedure to ensure that all fiduciary accounts are reviewed annually, as required by Regulation 9."

Write Concretely and Descriptively

A cliche or an ambiguous opening sentence does nothing more than fill up space on the page and state the obvious. Consider these lead sentences from audit comments:

> The following exceptions were noted.
>
> Some weaknesses exist in loan documentation.
>
> We identified the following deficiencies.
>
> Loan documentation needs improvement.
>
> Account records are not properly controlled.
>
> Controls are not adequate over processing.
>
> The process is not functioning effectively.
>
> During our review, it was noted that . . .

These sentences simply identify the topic of the narrative. Phrases such as "some exceptions," "control weaknesses," and "needs improvement" state the obvious and are seldom necessary. This is, after all, an audit report, and comments presented usually focus on lack of control. Opening lines such as these also offer little concrete substance. They are vague and hard to envision, "Needs improvement" or "not properly controlled" can mean many different things to many readers. Their ambiguity weakens their impact. Finally, these lines become predictable when they are overused. If readers get accustomed to seeing these phrases, they will begin to skip over them, looking for something they haven't read before.

Weak as these vague sentences are, writers find it hard to break the habit of using cliches. These sentences are safe, comfortable, and easy to write. When faced with a blank sheet of paper, an auditor can easily fill a few lines by starting out: "During our review of account balances, it was noted that balancing procedures need improvement." More creative and concrete substitutes are harder to write. If boilerplate phrases help you get started putting your first draft on paper, then by all means use them as you compose. Just be sure to go back and edit them out as soon as your thoughts are on paper.

Let's look again at our earlier examples. In Example 2, we need a rewrite of the standard phrase, "The results of our tests noted the following." An alternative is: "Applicants are not notified of credit decisions within 30 days, as required by Regulation B." In Example 3, "Procedures for reporting operating expenses should be improved" can be written more descriptively as "Operating expenses are misstated by $ 87,250."

Make your opening line specific and unique. Express your key message by answering this question: "In one sentence, what is the most important thing I have to say about this subject?"

Use Terms Your Readers Understand

Esoteric or excessively technical language will turn readers away as quickly as the cliches described above. For example, "In DB2, the activities of users with ABCADM and BCDADM authority have no audit trail." Readers perceive unfamiliar terms as a barrier between themselves and the writer. If they do not grasp the exact meaning of the sentence, they will probably expect the rest of the narrative to be equally difficult to follow.

When you need to use technical or possibly unknown terms in your comments, you must define them for the reader, but not necessarily with a standard definition. For instance, the writer of the "DB2" sentence, when asked to clarify, wrote: "ABCADM gives users access to all data within DB2, while BCDADM gives users access to certain data within an identified data base." That does give meaning to the acronyms, but it does not draw attention. When you are using technical terms, consider these options for describing them:

31

- State your conclusion using the term, then define it. ("Activities of users with ABCADM and BCDADM authority are not tracked. These authorities allow access to all information within a data base.")

- Define the term within the opening sentence. ("Activities of users with ABCADM and BCDADM authority, granting access to all information within a data base, are not tracked.")

- Use simpler language. ("Activities of users with the highest access authority are not tracked.")

Even when the language is not technical, writers may forget that terms are not familiar to all readers. For instance, consider this sentence: "Form 1166 is not completed for all personnel transfers." A more easily understood revision might be: "Personnel transfers are sometimes communicated by phone, and not put in writing."

As you begin to compose, start thinking more about your reader and less about your own work. Recognize that your audit process and logic follow a research pattern, not a reporting pattern. Step out of the logic you have used in fieldwork and begin responding to the logic your readers will apply to the report. Responding to the readers' logic, as outlined in Exhibit 3-2, will get your narrative off to a strong start.

EXHIBIT 3-2

AUDITOR'S LOGIC	READER'S LOGIC
What is the control?	What are the results?
How should it be tested?	What are the problems?
How well is the control working?	How big is the problem?
What exceptions or control weaknesses exist?	Why does it matter?
	How did this happen?
What should be done?	What has been done or will be done to correct this?

Choose the Information of Greatest Interest to Your Reader

Varying your opening sentences to suit both the occasion and the reader will make your reports more interesting and more persuasive. While we have emphasized the value of stating the conclusion, or results, at the start of comments, other elements may be more effective under certain circumstances.

What is judged to be the most important idea may vary from one occasion to the next. Here are several versions of the same comment, each with a different beginning.

FUNDS TRANSFER

Version 1

Funds-transfer authorization cards for four corporate account holders were incomplete, showing the names of authorized callers but lacking the confidential identification numbers. For two other accounts, new names had been added to the cards, but authorization letters were not in the files.

These cards are relied on in transferring up to four million dollars a day among accounts. Accuracy is essential to ensure that only authorized changes are made to the Bank's records of individuals allowed to authorize funds transfers.

The Funds Transfer Department should confirm receipt and verify the completeness and correctness of all new or revised authorized caller cards.

Version 2

Changes to authorization cards for funds transfers are required to be documented by authorization letters from the account holder, and revised cards must show complete information, including confidential identification numbers of authorized callers.

Our review of these cards showed that four of them included the names of authorized callers but did not include the confidential identification numbers. For two other accounts, new names had been added to the cards, but authorization letters were not in the files.

The Funds Transfer Department does not acknowledge receipt or confirm the correctness of revised authorized caller cards, which are relied on in transferring as much as four million dollars a day.

The department should confirm receipt and verify the completeness and correctness of all new or revised authorized caller cards.

Version 3

Incomplete funds-transfer authorization cards allow the potential for fraudulent requests to be processed. Four cards did not include the confidential identification numbers, and two accounts were missing authorization letters for names added to the cards. Four million dollars a day are transferred on the basis of information on these authorization cards.

The Funds Transfer Department does not acknowledge receipt or confirm the correctness of revised cards.

The department should confirm receipt and verify the completeness and correctness of all new or revised authorized caller cards.

Version 4

The Funds Transfer Department does not acknowledge receipt or confirm the correctness of revised authorized caller cards, resulting in incomplete records. These cards are relied on in transferring as much as four million dollars a day.

Authorization cards for four corporate account holders showed the names of authorized callers, but did not include the confidential identification numbers. For two other accounts, new names had been added to the cards, but authorization letters were not in the files. We recommend that Funds Transfer confirm all changes with the corporate account holder.

Version 5

Funds Transfer should confirm all changes to authorized caller cards with the corporate account holder. This will help prevent fraudulent transfers being initiated and processed and will ensure the validity of authorized caller information.

The Funds Transfer Department does not acknowledge receipt or confirm the correctness of revised authorized caller cards, resulting in incomplete records. These cards are relied on in transferring as much as four million dollars a day.

Authorization cards for four corporate account holders showed the names of authorized callers, but did not include the confidential identification numbers. For two other accounts, new names had been added to the cards, but authorization letters were not in the files.

These five versions differ not only stylistically, but also strategically. The emphasis, tone, and message vary from one comment to another. Any one may be appropriate, depending on several variable factors. Your job as an effective writer is to choose the approach that is right for your situation.

Analysis of the Five Versions

VERSION 1

Version 1 begins with the facts, the results of testing. This follows the outline of the attention-getting opening we used earlier in this chapter. This is a direct opening that calls attention to the issue.

Advantages. Describing the condition in the first sentence draws your reader into the narrative. It wastes no space or time, and allows the reader to browse through your report, reviewing the opening line of each comment to learn your key points.

Disadvantages. Some auditors find this approach too blunt. If the condition presents a problem, this opening line will almost always be written in a negative tone.

Appropriate Uses. Starting with the conclusion is the most versa-tile form of organization. Because it is the approach most readers expect and prefer, it can be effective for most comments, except where there is a need to soften the tone.

VERSION 2

Version 2 begins with criteria, stating the policies applicable to funds transfer. No judgment or conclusion is offered in the first sentence. Instead, the writer sets the stage by describing the required procedures.

Advantages. This opening overcomes the drawback of beginning with the statement of a problem by using objective, factual language in the opening lines. Citing a requirement, policy, or regulation first establishes the authority and validity of the point that follows.

Disadvantages. There is seldom much exciting material in a policy or regulation, so this opening may seem uninteresting. Some readers may believe that the writer is telling them what they already know, and entrepreneurial-minded managers may dismiss the emphasis on rules and regulations as insignificant.

Appropriate Uses. When your review is strictly to encourage compli-ance or when regulations are extremely important, the criteria-first strategy may be effective. If the reader is likely to resist a strongly worded conclusion, this structure may give an impression of greater objectivity, distancing the writer from any judgment of the facts. Finally, in a highly compliance-oriented environment, this may be the presentation management prefers.

VERSION 3

Version 3 highlights the effect of the situation, showing immedi-ately why incomplete authorization cards pose a risk to the bank.

Advantages. Beginning with the effect creates the strongest tone of these five beginnings. It shows the business significance of the situation, and grabs the attention of senior management.

Disadvantages. While the writer using this technique may impress senior management, he or she will not win friends among line managers. If given a choice of the five versions of the sample comment, the Funds Transfer manager would not be likely to pick Version 3. Used inappropriately, this technique can exaggerate the significance of a finding.

Appropriate Uses. Significant findings can be presented effectively using this format. The stronger tone sets apart this comment from the others in the report, highlighting its importance. At times, you may want to use this strong approach deliberately to attract senior management to an issue. Perhaps it is a significant item on which line management will not take action or a widespread issue that needs the executives' attention.

VERSION 4

Version 4 starts by identifying the cause of incomplete authorization cards and describes specific examples of the problem in the second paragraph.

Advantages. Stating the cause of a problem first may point the way to a solution. It focuses on the underlying problem, not the symptoms.

Disadvantages. If you have not carefully analyzed the situation, your identification of cause may be perceived as judgmental or as a conclusion without facts to support it. If the cause is obvious, your emphasis on it will appear simplistic.

Appropriate Uses. Begin with the cause when you have identified a fundamental procedural weakness. If you have tested your recommendation and are confident that the answer to the problem lies in eliminating what you have identified as the cause, use this structure to prepare the reader for the recommended solution.

VERSION 5

Version 5 offers the recommendation first, followed by the potential benefit.

Advantages. Stating a recommendation and its benefit uses positive language and will soften the tone of the opening. Highlighting the recommendation first can also make your report structure more action-oriented, focusing on possible solutions rather than existing problems.

Disadvantages. Readers unaccustomed to this style may interpret the report as telling management what should be done. To counter this tone, the recommendation can be written to avoid the word "should." The recommendation and benefit can be put together in one sentence such as, "Confirming all changes to authorized caller cards will help prevent fraudulent transfers being initiated and processed and will ensure the validity of authorized caller information."

Appropriate Uses. In a consultative report, this style is appropriate to present recommendations for solutions to problems you were asked to help solve. Stressing recommendations and benefits can also contribute to a more positive, constructive tone in your reporting.

The worksheet shown in Exhibit 3-3 can help you choose the appropriate tone for an opening.

Design Your Opening to Guide the Reader

Opening sentences express your key points and help guide readers through a report, making it easy for them to find the most important information at the start of every comment. You can further guide the reader by using headings, different typefaces, and other design elements to highlight your topics.

A heading for each comment can indicate your subject or express your message about that subject. Types of headings include:

Topic Only: Loan Documentation

Expanded Topic: Procedures for Maintaining Loan Documentation

EXHIBIT 3-3

CHOOSING YOUR STRATEGIC OPENING

A Checklist for Decision-Making

1. How significant is the issue?

   A. Minor   B. Major

2. What is management's likely reaction?

   A. Accepting   B. Resistant

3. Whose attention do you want to get?

   A. Line   B. Senior

4. How would you describe the reader you want to influence?

   A. Sensitive   B. Tough

   A = Soften the tone.   B = Use a stronger tone.

Conclusion: Incomplete Loan Documentation

Recommendation: Maintain Complete Loan
                               Documentation

Headings expressing conclusions or recommendations give readers a complete overview of the content. Headings may also be used to produce a summary or table of contents.

Another technique for highlighting key messages is to format the sentence of conclusion differently from the rest of the narrative. You might use underlining or bold type, or you might indent and set apart sentences to draw the readers' attention.

<u>The Funds Transfer Department does not acknowledge receipt or confirm the correctness of revised authorized caller cards.</u>

The Funds Transfer Department does not acknowledge receipt or confirm the correctness of revised authorized caller cards.

The Funds Transfer Department does not acknowledge receipt or confirm the correctness of revised authorized caller cards.

> Authorization cards for four corporate account holders showed the names of authorized callers but did not include the confidential identification numbers.

In addition to your topic heading, you may want to use a subheading to label the recommendation. This formatting allows readers to easily find both the problem and the solution for every point you present. Here is an example:

Authorized Caller Cards Not Verified

The Funds Transfer Department does not acknowledge receipt or confirm the correctness of authorized caller cards, resulting in incomplete records. These cards are relied on in transferring as much as four million dollars a day.

Authorization cards for four corporate account holders showed the names of authorized callers, but did not include the confidential identification numbers. For two other accounts, new names had been added to the cards, but authorization letters were not in the files.

Recommendation

Confirm all changes to authorized caller cards with the corporate account holder.

Changes in the format, such as bold type or underlining, can be especially useful if you need to include a few sentences of explanation or background information in the first paragraph of your comment. Instead of opening the comment with this description, which many readers find uninteresting, you can preface it with your conclusion, highlighted for the reader. An illustration follows.

Compliance with Regulation 9

The unit does not have a reconciliation procedure to ensure that all fiduciary accounts are reviewed annually.

Regulation 9 requires that assets held in a fiduciary account be reviewed annually and within 15 months of the last review. The "Assets Under Management" report lists all fiduciary accounts managed.

Long comments, those of a page or more, need to be especially well designed to catch and hold the readers' attention. After the heading, you might begin with a summary paragraph, presenting key elements such as conclusion, effect, and cause. This lets the reader know what to expect in the rest of the narrative and gives an overview for busy readers who are skimming through the report. Each paragraph that follows should cover one subject and should start with a topic sentence expressing the key idea covered. Subheadings may also be useful.

Heading
Background
Finding
Recommendation

These simple formatting techniques can increase the readability of your report, make it more inviting to the reader, and ensure that all recipients will learn your most important ideas.

With direct, concise writing and good design features, your reports will stand out among the others in managers' in-boxes. Work to get your readers' attention so that they will not have to work at finding your message. Remember to:

- State your conclusion directly.

- Write concretely and descriptively.

- Use terms your readers understand.

- Choose the information of greatest interest to the reader.

- Design your openings to guide the reader.

4

Managing Detail

Audit trainees are usually surprised when they see their first set of workpapers and the resulting report, not because they see something unexpected in the content, organization, or logic, but because they see a dramatic difference in volume between the workpapers and the report. "What happened to all the work and documentation?" is a common response. "How can a three-inch set of workpapers be reduced to a six-page report?"

The judgment on how much supporting data to include in the report is one of the most difficult challenges facing new auditors and writers. The choice of amount and type of detail included is based partially on logic and partially on emotion. Auditors are trained to document the detail of their testing and analysis, and they feel that they need to hold onto these data. When it comes time to write, auditors often want to transfer the complexity of their auditing, as documented in the workpapers, to the report. They may want to show the extent of their testing by describing what they did and what they learned. In an attempt to anticipate and respond to every question or objection the reader may raise, they provide detailed explanations and complete supporting data. Perhaps they have been conditioned in school or in other jobs to believe that the bigger the report, the more work it represents. In business, and especially in internal auditing, that does not hold true.

Managers demand concise presentations, yet they do not want a document so terse that it leaves important questions unanswered.

Your job is to balance the need for evidence with the need for conciseness. You must select just the right amount of supporting detail for your report and present it in a readable style.

To write a targeted report with the right amount of detail, you need to:

- Consider your audience and purpose.

- Summarize supporting data.

- Select convincing and useful information.

- Assess the value of information.

- Present data in a readable style.

Consider Your Audience and Purpose

Auditors often write with their own boss in mind—the audit supervisor, manager, or director. This leads them to present data in much the same format and at much the same level as they would in their workpapers. That level, though, is generally too detailed for the report. Audit management should evaluate the substance and validity of the work and the appropriateness of conclusions and recommendations by reviewing workpapers, not report drafts. The time to pass judgment on these issues is earlier in the review process. The report draft should represent agreement already reached between auditor and supervisor. Auditors who write for their bosses tend to include too much information, and then become frustrated by having to rewrite or eliminate sections of their report.

Focusing on the true audiences—line and senior management—does not provide a magical answer to the question of supporting data, either. Writers directing themselves to line management may include all the supporting evidence, including the detailed list of exceptions and an explanation of the extent of audit testing done. In fact, line management should already have this information. When presenting findings, during the audit or at the closing conference, the auditor covers this detail, usually presenting a copy of the audit worksheet. The manager already has the information needed to correct the exceptions and may only expect a summary of the data in the report to document the issue.

Senior management has varying needs and expectations. In some companies, senior management wants none of the detail, looking only for a conclusion and a digest of the supporting points; in others, management wants to know more. Your knowledge of the audience

44

in your organization is critical to making an effective judgment on the amount of information in your report. If you are not certain of their needs and interests, talk to the senior managers who receive your reports. Find out if they are using the information you present, and if they are satisfied with its presentation. If you have a variety of preferences among your senior managers, make the detail optional for your readers by placing it in appendices, exhibits, or clearly labeled separate sections.

As you construct the content of your report, keep in mind your purposes. The report's job is not to educate uninformed readers of operating procedures or concepts of internal control, nor to justify the audit work done. The report is the summary of your work, informing management of significant results and pointing the way to action. Design your report to accomplish these higher-level objectives.

Summarize Supporting Data

Audit worksheets are organized to correspond to the sequence of testing, not necessarily the order of presenting results. To make an effective bridge between the workpapers and the report, you must summarize and reorganize the worksheets.

The steps in making this analysis are:

1. Look for common topics or themes.

2. Group similar items.

3. Look for the underlying problem or control weakness.

4. Draw a conclusion from the data.

5. Select examples from the detailed data to support the conclusion.

6. Organize data in order of importance.

Exhibits 4-1 and 4-2 illustrate these analytical steps. Exhibit 4-1 represents the worksheets from a section of a purchasing audit. As the auditor analyzes the information, he or she may label and organize the material as shown in Exhibit 4-2.

Notice that as the auditor goes through this analysis, the data become more focused. There are fewer numbers and more narrative

EXHIBIT 4-1

Example of Audit Worksheets

Testing of Purchase Orders

Long-Form P.O.s (Over $5,000.00)

Population: 1,320   Sample Size: 140

P.O. #	Vendor	Date	Amount	Date Rec.	Bids	Mgr. Appr.
1346	Acme	3/2	5,500	3/20	—	x
1572	Widget	3/4	10,643	3/18	—	x
1816	Ace	3/15	12,125	—	x	x
1866	Global	3/18	8,389	4/6	x	x
1901	Acme	3/19	11,987	—	—	x
1967	Baker	3/21	15,000	—	—	x

Testing of Purchase Orders

Short-Form P.O.s (Under $5,000.00)

Population: 1,450   Sample Size: 98

P.O. #	Vendor	Date	Amount	Date Rec.	Mgr. Appr.
2118	Ace	3/3	1,250	3/12	x
2167	Jones	3/8	765	—	x
2211	Acme	3/11	4,450	3/30	Over limit
2287	Blake	3/18	4,750	—	Over limit
2331	Global	3/21	3,250	4/20	x
2356	Baker	3/22	1,854	4/12	x

EXHIBIT 4-2

Example of Summarized Supporting Data

Summary of Purchase Order Testing

Objective: To determine if purchase orders are properly issued and approved before buying merchandise, if prices and bids are obtained before purchase, and if receipt of merchandise is properly recorded.

Scope: 98 short-form purchase orders and140 long-form purchase orders completed between April 1 and May 1, 19xx.

Results:

Summary of Long-Form P. O. s

April 1- May 1, 19xx

	# of Exceptions	# of Total Samples
— Date merchandise received was not noted	63	45.0
— No price listed on P. O.	11	7.8
— No bids attached or examined	64	45.7
— Merchandise received before P. O. was issued	72	51.4

Summary of Long-Form P. O. s

April 1- May 1, 19xx

	# of Exceptions	# of Total Samples
— Date merchandise received was not noted	42	42.8
— No price listed on P. O.	16	16.3
— No bids attached or examined	7	7.1
— Merchandise received before P. O. was issued	13	13.3

Conclusion: Purchase orders are not properly completed and approved and prices and bids are not obtained before purchases are made.

explaining what the numbers mean. The specifics (names of vendors, numbers of purchase orders) fall away and an overview of the situation emerges.

Once the auditor draws the conclusion, the data must be reorganized in order of importance. That does not mean that the largest number of exceptions comes first. Items representing the largest risk, greatest exposure, or biggest problem are given priority, followed by the other items in descending order of significance. In our example, the statistics on "Date merchandise received was not noted" do not represent the most significant finding from the testing. The largest risk items are the lack of bids and prices before the purchase of merchandise, since these exceptions could result in overpricing or unauthorized purchasing.

Worksheets such as those shown in Exhibit 4-1 sometimes do make their way into the audit report. Most often they appear as an itemized listing of exceptions. The data are raw, detailed, and unanalyzed. Itemizations present one exception after another. They can be recognized by the following common structure:

> During our review of documentation for 20 loans, we noted the following:
>
> 1. Current insurance could not be located in the files for: A. Smith, #01111; P. Andrews, #10222; and C. Jones, #01333.
>
> 2. Lien receipts could not be located for: P. Andrews, #10222; L. Wise, # 20345; and T. Thomas, # 12789.
>
> 3. Power of Attorney forms were not properly completed for C. Adams, # 23122; and T. Thomas, # 12789.
>
> 4. Security section of the note was not completed for A. Jackson, # 22112.

This represents lazy writing and is not an effective presentation for a management report. It is little more than a copy of the detail documented in the workpapers.

Select Convincing and Useful Information

One problem in summarizing audit results is that writers may be too concise, describing the problem but not offering enough information to support the conclusion or show the significance.

Examples of auditors' selection of information for the purchasing comment illustrate how the use of data can influence the persuasiveness and tone of a narrative.

EXAMPLE 1

More guidelines are needed in the initial stages of the purchasing process to prevent forms being received and accepted with limited information. Also, it was learned several purchases were not completed in a timely manner.

EXAMPLE 2

The purchase order process is not being properly administered.

Purchase orders are:

- incomplete,

- not promptly issued,

- unsubstantiated,

- not monitored, and

- not properly authorized.

These two versions are certainly concise, but they offer vague, unsupported generalizations. The first is so general that readers cannot envision what the problem is, let alone the extent of that problem.

"Limited information" is an ambiguous phrase. Readers do not know what is missing from the forms (will they assume they are purchase orders?) or how important that missing information is. "Several purchases were not completed in a timely manner" is equally indefinite. Is "timely" ten days, thirty days, or some other length of time?

In the second version, the problems are enumerated, but in unclear language. "Incomplete" tells us no more than "limited information." "Unsubstantiated" and "not properly authorized" are open to interpretation.

Another writer was more specific in the opening line, but used ambiguous language as support.

> Purchase orders are not being properly approved or executed as to price, quantity, quality, and vendor. We noted that a significant percentage of the long-form purchase orders were not supported by competitive bids. We also noted that many short-form purchase orders exceed the limit of the approving officer's authority.

Yet another used statistics, but not very effectively.

> A review of the open order file disclosed 288 exceptions in the 2770 orders processed in April.

Writers who balance a summary statement of conclusion with concise but specific data best achieve the goals of providing support and showing significance. The following example is clear, yet brief.

> Almost half of the 140 purchase orders we tested were missing, incomplete, or provided incorrect information.
>
> Specifically:
>
> • Bids were not obtained in 46% of the cases.
>
> • Merchandise was received before the purchase order was issued 51% of the time.
>
> • Prices were missing on 12% of the purchase orders.

Other information besides the summary of audit results that auditors may consider including in their reports includes descriptions of operating procedures, audit procedures, and recommendations. Any information you include in the report should meet at least one of these criteria:

• Provides support for the conclusion.

- Shows the significance of the problem.

- Allows for corrective action.

We have already seen how a concise summary of the audit results provides support for the conclusion. Examples of the other types of information will help determine how much is appropriate for the report.

Operating Procedures

Writers believe that readers unfamiliar with the area reported on need descriptions of the operations in order to understand the points presented in the report, so they tend to give a step-by-step or chronological description. Here is an example:

> The Payroll Section uses Basic Employee Data forms to process new employee data into the payroll system. These forms are filled out by HRD's Employment Section and contain personal employee data (employee name, employee identification number, Social Security number, birth date, etc.) as well as job-related data (job title code and base hours). HRD's Employment Section forwards these forms to the Payroll Section for processing and filing. We noted that four of the Basic Employee Data forms completed in the last month had incorrect job title codes. Payroll did not act as a control by correcting the codes on the forms before entering them into the payroll system.

Senior management hardly needs the detailed description of the Basic Employee Data form and its processing. The name of the form speaks for itself, and so the description is superfluous. What the readers need to know about the topic can be incorporated into the conclusion:

> Four of the Basic Employee Data forms completed by HRD last month showed incorrect job titles. These were not identified and corrected by Payroll before the new employee data was entered into the payroll system.

In writing the comment from the purchasing worksheets presented in this chapter, one auditor began this way:

> Purchasing procedures require that purchases of merchandise be supported by a properly authorized purchase order. Procurement is responsible for ensuring that the purchase order includes the description, quantity, price, and related information for the commodities to be purchased. Company policy requires that procurements in excess of $5,000 be approved by specified company officers; use the long-form purchase order; and be supported by written vendor bids. Furthermore, the date of receipt for goods is required to be recorded on all purchase orders.

Such detailed operating descriptions are not needed to support the conclusion, as long as the message is clear. Neither do such descriptions show the significance of the problem. Although they do reinforce the validity of your conclusion by citing the policies and requirements of purchasing, it is not necessary to spell them out in such detail. You can expect your readers to have a general understanding of purchasing requirements. Where you need to refer to a relevant company policy, you can do so by including it in your statement of the problem. For example: "Thirteen percent of purchase orders exceeded the officer's approval limit specified by company policy."

Some writers argue that these details meet the third criterion we outlined above, allowing for corrective action. Management needs these details, they argue, so they will know exactly how to fix the problem. Remember, management already has this information. They are, after all, running the operation you are describing, and you have already discussed these matters with line management before writing the report. Do not be condescending to readers by telling them what they already know.

Audit Procedures

A common belief is that we need to explain what testing we did and how we arrived at our conclusion in order for readers to accept our findings. As a result, paragraphs such as the following often appear in audit comments.

> The auditors reviewed transactions and related documentation, on a sample basis, for purchase orders issued by the

Purchasing Department. The sample of purchase orders reviewed was selected from those issued from April 1 through May 1, 19xx. The auditors reviewed 140 long-form purchase orders, for purchases over $5,000, of the 1,320 issued during the audit period. The auditors also reviewed 98 short-form purchase orders, for purchases $5,000 or under, of the 1,450 issued during the period.

The significant information from this paragraph is the number of purchase orders in the sample (140 and 98) and the time covered (April 1 - May 1). These data are needed to show the significance of the exceptions that follow (63 of 140, 16 of 98, etc.) and to give perspective on how frequently the problems occur (all within one month). The rest is filler.

When describing a sample size, state the information as concisely as possible to keep the readers' attention focused on the information they are most interested in—the audit results. If possible, make an indirect reference to the sample size, as we showed above ("13 of 98 purchase orders tested exceeded the officer's approval limit").

Too much emphasis on audit procedures may convey a defensive tone. Talking too much about your sample size and testing techniques may make it appear that you are justifying your work, or it may serve to cushion the results that follow the description of procedures. By starting with a "safe" paragraph on testing procedures, you are able to hide the results, presenting them one or two paragraphs into the page rather than in the first lines.

Sometimes auditors describe their testing even when they have nothing to report on the item, except that "no exceptions were noted." The result is a report focusing primarily on what the auditor did. This happens most often when a standard report format is used, perhaps in a branch audit. Here is a brief excerpt from one such report:

DEPOSITS

Withdrawal tickets were checked for proper signatures and approvals. Requests were made for signed withdrawal orders for all withdrawals with missing signatures. Closed account verifications were sent out on a daily basis. Balances in all general ledger deposit accounts were proved to the recaps as of January 29, February 28, and March 31. Savings, DDA, and Certificate trial balances were proved to the recaps. No exceptions were noted.

The rest of the report continued in the same style. After revision, what the writer had originally presented as six pages of such descriptions was revised into two pages, outlining the scope of items covered in the branch audit, concluding on positive items (those with "no exceptions"), and describing the few weaknesses identified.

Recommendations

Recommendations are necessary to point the way to corrective action. Styles of presenting recommendations range from the step-by-step prescription of required action to a statement of the desired result. Your choice of detail in the recommendation will depend on the depth of your analysis, the image you choose to present, and the discussions you have had with management before issuing the report.

Let's review examples of the extremes. First, the step-by-step outline:

As per company policy, the date material is received in the stockroom should be stamped on the purchase order by quality control evidencing receipt of the goods. The supervisor of the storeroom should review and approve receipts and P.O.s on a daily basis prior to forwarding the approved P.O. to the accounting department. The storeroom should not accept delivery of any item for which there is no purchase order outstanding. As required by policy, all purchases in excess of $5,000 require bids. The director of the Purchasing Department should review and approve all bids accepted by the Company. Accounts Payable should only pay on those invoices for which there is an approved P.O., invoice, and quality control checklist on file. Internal audit also recommends P.O.'s #12345 and 38567 be voided and reordered via the proper purchasing procedures. In addition, P.O.'s #65487 and 78632 should be closed out, and P.O.'s #54321 and 58672 approved by the requesting department after quality control has examined the items.

Now, a broad and concise recommendation:

> Procurement should enhance their review of purchase orders to ensure compliance with current purchasing procedures.

The first detailed recommendation sounds as if the auditor is reprimanding or dictating solutions. The second is so vague that it appears as if the auditor has not spent much time developing an appropriate solution.

A recommendation answers these questions: What needs to be done to fix the existing condition? What can be done to prevent the problem from happening again? The recommendation you present in your report may address one or both of these questions. In some companies, when the reported condition has already been discussed with management and resolved, the published recommendation will focus only on the second question—how to prevent a problem from recurring. In others, the report will include both parts of the recommendation.

In making the decision what to include in your recommendation, determine whether you want to emphasize corrective or preventive action. Remember that corrective action is limited; it fixes the reported problems but may not do anything to guard against these problems in the future. Preventive action addresses the underlying cause. A more results-oriented audit report will emphasize preventive actions. It will, as one general auditor describes it, "treat the problem, not the symptoms."

Some possible preventive actions in the purchasing example might be establishing purchasing procedures, independently reviewing purchase orders, and training purchasing agents in required procedures and monitoring their performance.

To make a recommendation measurable, express it in terms of the desired result. What is the control objective that needs to be met? What criteria will be applied to evaluate compliance? One auditor, for example, stated the recommendation as follows.

> Procedures should be established to ensure that competitive bids are obtained and filed, that all prices and vendor terms are included on the purchase order, and that the appropriate level of management reviews the purchase order before it is issued. A comparison should be made of goods received to a copy of the purchase order to ensure that only requested goods and services are received. Also, before paying vendors,

> purchase order, receiving report, and invoices should be compared.

This gives enough detail for management to take action and auditors to evaluate compliance without specifying "who-should-do-what-when" as the first example does.

Another auditor wrote this preventive-action recommendation:

> The requestor should obtain an approved purchase order before ordering goods or services. Purchasing should verify the order for appropriate price and use of an approved vendor. Purchasing should select and keep a list of approved vendors based on their competitive bids, payment history, and reliability.

Remember that the recommendation you write for the report draft represents a negotiable solution to be agreed on by line management. Writing a detailed, step-by-step recommendation makes the actions appear as orders: "This is what you shall do." There is little room for management's involvement in solving the problem. On the other hand, writing a vague recommendation may leave your position undefined. When management offers proposed solutions, how will you evaluate whether the proposal "enhances control?" Such open-ended statements may cause you to accept less than is required to prevent the problem, because in fact almost any action would "enhance control."

Focusing on desired results allows you to define the expected solution and describe how the effectiveness of proposed actions will be measured. It also has the advantage of allowing room for management to suggest their own procedures to meet the desired goal.

After having reached agreement with management, you will have agreement on three additional items: action steps, target date, and person responsible. You can incorporate these into the report by including the information in management's response following the recommendation, or you can substitute the new action steps or solutions for the initial recommendation.

As you evaluate the need for information—results, procedures, operating descriptions, and recommendations—judge each element from the readers' perspective. Are the data necessary to support the conclusion, illustrate significance, or allow for corrective action? This is the information readers will be looking for. Other details will diminish the value and readability of the report.

Assess the Value of Information

The cost of reporting every exception you identify can far outweigh the value of bringing some items to senior management's attention. The time it takes for you to write and for management to read and respond to such a report may be costly. For instance, the following items were included in audit reports:

> Travelers checks fee expense of $10.00 was not recorded in July.
>
> A difference of $99.79 in the constant payment proof could not be identified.
>
> A retirement cake was purchased with company funds.
>
> Numerous car wash invoices did not properly identify the vehicle.

The insignificance of the amounts not only inflates the dollar cost of reporting them, but may also cause the auditor to pay a price in his or her relationship with management. Reporting this information contributes to the perception that auditors look for minor problems. These items can be easily pointed out to management orally and do not need to clutter the report.

Sometimes, many small problems add up to a bigger control weakness, and so you have reason to present these in your report. When you do, focus on the bigger control weakness and consolidate the itemized exceptions.

The following version of a comment on open purchase orders shows how too much detail detracts from the value of the message.

> Our review identified seven purchase orders that have been open for an unusually long period of time. Discussions disclosed the following information:
>
> 1. Vendors did not recognize two purchase orders (#12345 and 34567). Purchasing reordered the goods on 4/30.

2. Although a department cancelled P.O. 65487, no one removed the P.O. from the open file.

3. Purchasing records indicated that P.O. 54321 and 58672 were open; however, the requesting departments informed purchasing that they had received the material.

A more valuable comment concentrates on the control weakness.

The Purchasing Department has no way of readily identifying obsolete or cancelled purchase orders, nor do they receive a report listing outstanding purchase orders by date. We identified three purchase orders that were in the active file but had been cancelled or completed.

As a final test for the information you include in the report, assess its value. Determine what it contributes to the improved operation of the unit, to the performance of the organization, and to your role and relationship with management.

Present Data in a Readable Style

Once you have chosen the appropriate information, you must make the data easy to read and understand. In the next paragraph, an auditor has good statistics, but makes it difficult for the reader to comprehend them.

Routines for ensuring timely write-off of uncollectable balances required improvement in that my review of 40 accounts ($225,000) selected statistically from 518 accounts ($1,012,000) written off during the year disclosed that (a) intervals between most recent collection activity and recommendation for write-off had ranged from 33 to 180 days (average 96 day) in 13 instances ($32,000 - 12%); (b) intervals between most recent previous activity had ranged from 20 to 123 days (average 50 days) in six instances ($29,000 - 10%); and (c) default letters had not been issued from 100 to 250 days (average 135 days) in seven instances ($37,000 - 9%).

Formatting techniques for increasing the readability of data include using:

- numbers and percentages,
- bulleted items or numerical listings,
- tables or charts, and
- exhibits or attachments.

Numbers and percentages. While quantification provides excellent support for the conclusion, too many numbers can be hard for the reader to absorb, as shown in the previous example. The most succinct way to present data is to mention the sample size once and then express the findings in numbers or percentages. Generally, percentages are easier to understand than numbers alone, but you must use your judgment to determine which presentation makes a stronger statement. The following version presents the number of exceptions:

Of 140 purchases over $5,000, 64 were missing competitive bids, 72 were issued after the merchandise had been received, and 11 were missing the price.

An alternative presentation is to use percentages. For example:

Testing showed that bids had not been prepared for 46% of the purchases, and 51% of the merchandise was received before the purchase order was issued. Also, prices were not included on 8% of the purchase orders prepared, and 45% lacked the date of receipt. These results are based on a sample of 140 purchase orders over $5,000.

Bulleted items or numerical listings. Listing the major points or exceptions in bulleted lists not only makes data easy to understand but also highlights the points you want to emphasize. The following example calls the readers' attention to the nature of the exceptions.

Approximately half of the purchase orders reviewed were processed with one or more of the following errors:

- Bids not attached.
- Price not listed.
- Merchandise received before the P. O. was issued.
- Order exceeded the officer's limit.

Another version makes the numbers easy to understand by presenting them as bulleted items.

Approximately half of the purchase orders reviewed were incomplete:

- 46% of long-form purchase orders did not have bids.
- 72% of large purchases and 7% of smaller purchases were made before the purchase order was issued.
- 63% of long-form and 42% of short-form purchase orders did not show the date merchandise was received.

Tables or charts. Another way to present a listing of data is in an easy-to-read table or chart. When you use this format, keep it simple and label each column clearly. Be sure to precede the chart with a statement of its meaning.

In the following chart, the writer has summarized the data, but has made two common mistakes: the column labels are not precise, and each column presents more than one piece of information.

Exception	Long Form	Short Form
Merchandise ordered without P.O.	72/51%	7/7%
Receipt date omitted	63/45%	42/43%
No bid attached	64/46%	N/A
Price not shown	11/8%	16/16%

The next example defines the terms and presents each piece of information in a separate column.

Prices of merchandise were not properly obtained before purchases were made. A review of 140 purchases over $5,000 produced the following results.

60

Exception	Number	Percent of Sample
No bids	64	45%
Purchase made without P.O.	72	51%
No price	11	7%

Bar graphs can quickly display trends over time.

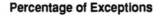

Percentage of Exceptions

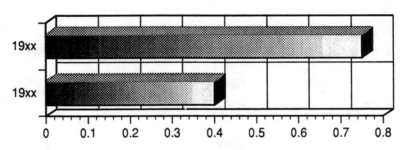

Pie charts easily divide the population or components.

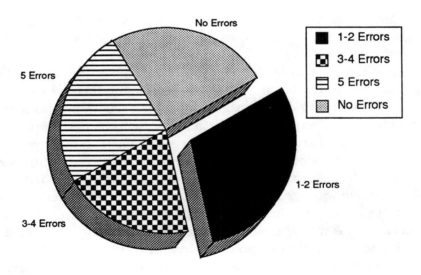

Exhibits or attachments. If you are addressing several audiences with different degrees of interest in the detail of your findings, you may present the data as an exhibit or attachment. Using any of the formatting techniques described above, you can position the information so that it is optional to the readers. Generally, any listing of data that is more than half a page long may be separated from the text. An exhibit appears within the body of the report, but on a separate page from the narrative. An attachment, or appendix, comes at the end of the report. When using either of these techniques, be sure you make a clear reference to the data within the text. You should describe the conclusion drawn from the data, refer to the number of the exhibit or attachment, and tell the reader where to find it. For example:

> Approximately half of the purchase orders reviewed were processed with one or more of the following errors:
>
> - Bids not attached.
> - Price not listed.
> - Merchandise received before the P.O. was issued.
> - Order exceeded the officer's limit.
>
> The number and types of exceptions are listed in Attachment 1 at the end of the report.

Careful use of numbers and percentages, presented in the appropriate format, will make your data more inviting and meaningful to your varied audiences.

An effective audit report offers solid and convincing support for the comments and recommendations, yet remains focused and concise. You can strategically manage detail in your report by considering your readers and responding to their needs. A succinct, concrete, and conclusive summary of your data can mean more to management than three pages of data you ask them to interpret. When you consider what information to include in the report, select data that will persuade your readers or help them take corrective action, and leave out details and descriptions that add unneeded length to the report. Assess the value of each piece of information you include, making sure it contributes positively to your conclusions and recommendations. Finally, make data easy to understand by presenting them in a readable format.

While these logical arguments can be made for limiting detail and writing succinctly, it may be psychologically difficult to exclude detail in the report. Writers may feel they need to present data to explain issues completely, document all work done, or ensure that action steps taken are complete and specific. The paradox is that senior managers, when asked what they want, rarely request more information. Audit departments that have changed the format or content of reports in response to management's feedback indicate that they have shortened reports, added executive summaries, or included management actions. Readers do not want to be less informed. They want to be more informed with less information.

Ultimately, the time you take to select and present the detail of your work succinctly will produce great time savings in reaching agreement and getting solutions to recommendations. You will hold your readers' interest throughout the report, point management's attention to the most significant issues, and provide answers to the questions of greatest substance.

WRITING TO PERSUADE

5

Getting Results from Your Audit Report

How do you measure the return on the time your audit team spends completing documentation and perfecting reports? Do you determine the value of the audit by the number of findings presented, the length of the report, or the size of the distribution list? Or do you assess audit's contribution according to the amount of loss or number of errors prevented, the size of savings or increased efficiencies identified, the practicality of recommendations, and the degree of management's acceptance?

If you score higher on the volume of paper you produce than on the results achieved from that paper production, your reports may be more informational than persuasive. Such informational report writing reflects an attitude that places responsibility for control consciousness on the shoulders of line management. The thinking is: "I present the facts. If management understands the importance of controls and compliance, they will act. If they don't accept the recommendation, it is because they are not control conscious, and it is their burden to live with the risk."

Persuasive writing starts with an attitude of understanding your readers, not of discounting their objections. When you approach report writing as a process of producing value rather than volume, you will be more likely to concentrate on presenting the business signifi-cance or risk of your comments or recommendations, and working toward management's acceptance and action. As a persuasive writer, you will remember that success is based not on the number of reports you write but on the value of the results and responses they get.

How do you accomplish these goals? Begin by positioning yourself to sell recommendations, not just present facts. Recognize that you cannot change the readers' outlook and initial objections, but remember that by understanding their priorities and showing the value of your recommendation in contributing to their goals, you can influence readers to change their point of view.

You can strengthen your reports' potential to get results by taking these steps:

- Describe and quantify the problem.
- Show the effect from management's point of view.
- Overcome objections.

Describe and Quantify the Problem

Every presentation of a recommendation, opinion, or argument must take into account the style in which the issue should be described. When broaching a sensitive subject with management, auditors and other analysts may choose to soften their approach by describing the problem indirectly.

The indirect presentation is prefaced by statements of scope, description of facts, and consideration of different interpretations. The conclusion and recommendation are voiced at the end of the discussion. Effective auditors often use this approach in meetings to counter resistance and build agreement step by step. The indirect style is preferable when management is hearing about a significant problem for the first time, when the recommendation is controversial or counter to other alternative solutions, or when the recipients are likely to be defensive or resistant.

By the time you write the audit report, line management should be well- informed of your facts, conclusions, and recommendations, and their resistance and defensiveness should be diminished. As a result of this preparatory work, the report can be more direct than your face-to-face discussions. The report, offering no surprises to line management, can summarize problems in a direct, succinct style. This is the manner of presentation most likely to get the attention of senior management, drawing them in to read your supporting information and recommendation.

In Chapter 3, we developed a model of "Heading—Conclusion—

Evidence" to capture and hold readers' interest. This organization is even more critical to persuasive writing, as it helps you avoid two common weaknesses in convincing an audience: unsupported generalizations and invalid conclusions.

Unsupported generalizations cause readers to reject the conclusion and recommendation. Without facts, data, or evidence to support points, a report is likely to cause controversy, alienate readers, or inflame issues. Consider management's likely reaction to the following comments.

> Office automation should be improved. The branch has purchased a number of personal computers that to date have been used primarily for word processing. Few analytical tools have been developed and the branch has not implemented automated applications for the numerous reports, schedules, and documentation being produced manually. We recommend that management identify tools and systems that could be automated.
>
> There is a problem with the timely clearing of overdrafts. Of the 20 largest overdrafts open on the audit date, eight had been open an unusually long period of time. Procedures should be developed to ensure more timely clearing of overdrafts.

The first example will lead to contradictory responses and counter-arguments. The branch manager might argue that the personal computers are in use 80% of the time, that in fact they were intended only for word processing, and that the manual reports and schedules take only about one day a month to produce. The manager's legitimate first reaction to the auditor's comment might be: "Where is your evidence that automation should be improved? How much of the time are the computers idle? How much time and paper can be saved by automating other reports?" The generalized comment and ambiguous recommendation deserve to be rejected. The logic of the argument is incomplete and cannot be expected to influence recipients.

The comment on overdrafts superficially offers some support for the conclusion, by citing the number of exceptions: eight out of twenty open overdrafts. Still, the critical supporting data is lacking. How large were the "largest" overdrafts? What is "an unusually long period of time?" The introductory statement, "There is a problem with the timely clearing of overdrafts," appears as the auditor's opinion, unsubstantiated by facts.

Not only must evidence be offered, but it must also be in sync with the conclusion. An invalid conclusion may overstate, understate, or misstate the facts. For example, an auditor wrote that "Account officers are exceeding their authorization limits. Seven percent of the fifty items reviewed were over the officer's limit." An exception rate of seven percent may hardly be large enough to draw such a broad conclusion. In contrast, it is possible to understate a conclusion. One auditor wrote: "Documentation exceptions existed in purchasing. Forty-eight percent of purchases over $5,000 were missing prices, and forty-two percent had no competitive bids." Lack of pricing and bids for such large purchases is much more than a "documentation exception." This language downplays the seriousness of the problem and stands in contrast to the data that follow.

Misstating the problem results when the writer focuses on the less significant data or confuses symptoms with causes. Sometimes an auditor will assume immediately that the item showing the greatest number of exceptions represents the biggest problem. As we saw in the purchasing examples in Chapter 4, this is not always the case. In those comments, writers who focused on missing dates of receipt ignored the bigger issues of pricing and purchasing authorization.

A more difficult judgment to make is the distinction between symptoms and causes. The open overdrafts in the example above may be just one symptom of a general lack of monitoring of customer accounts, or two incomplete authorization cards in funds transfer may be indicative of a larger control weakness of not verifying cards and the much greater exposure of unauthorized transfers.

The foundation of an effective persuasive document is a logical, well-supported conclusion. The Problem Analysis Worksheet in Exhibit 5-1 can help you think through complicated items, separating opinion from fact and distinguishing between symptoms and causes.

Once you have made a clear statement of the condition or problem, you must answer management's next question: "How big is it?" Knowing the size or extent of a problem helps management determine the severity and decide how much attention they want to give to the issue. Smaller exceptions or minor risks may be accepted, or the item may be delegated to a supervisor. When the issue is more material, or has a greater actual or potential effect on the business, higher management needs to be aware and involved.

EXHIBIT 5-1

Problem Analysis Worksheet

CONDITION

- What is the problem or opportunity?

- What evidence do you have of this?

CRITERIA

- What standard, policy, or procedure should be applied?

EFFECT

- What has been the actual or potential effect of the problem? (Give specific examples of cost, quality, timeliness, exposure, compliance, etc.)

- What is the benefit of making a change?

CAUSE

- What conditions, circumstances, or practices caused the situation or allowed it to occur?

- What fundamental weakness underlies this condition? Or: what can be done to prevent the problem?

RECOMMENDATION

- What needs to be done to solve the immediate problem?

- What can be put in place to prevent the problem from recurring?

- What is the cost of this recommendation?

- What benefits balance or outweigh the cost?

You can do this by avoiding generalizations and quantifying your conclusions. Most commonly, auditors quantify by giving the number of exceptions: "Forty-five percent of invoices examined were not signed by the manager." "Fourteen of thirty loan files were missing evidence of collateral." In addition to the number of exceptions, describing the size of the problem, other data may be helpful to put the item in perspective. Besides knowing the number of errors, a manager will want to consider the overall value or volume of the operation, unit, or function you are reporting on. For example, if the forty-five percent of unsigned invoices were over $10,000 each, the manager would be much more concerned than if they were each under $100. If all the total unsigned invoices represented $1,000,000 in purchases, the manager would take quicker action than for purchases representing $20,000. Similarly, a credit manager would want to know the value of the collateral for which there is no evidence.

As your report goes to higher levels of management, where readers are less familiar with the exact values of specific operations, such quantification may make the difference between an informative and a persuasive report. One auditor reported the following: "The amounts of fees for specialized customer services are not consistently collected." Had the writer quantified the total value of the fees, or the amount uncollected, readers would have been better able to judge the significance of the comment. As written, it blends into the body of the report all too easily, sounding very much like any other reported exception.

The writer can strengthen this comment by considering these questions: What does "not consistently collected" mean? Are fees assessed and collected arbitrarily, are they ignored under a certain dollar amount, or are they waived for large customers? Under what circumstances and how frequently are fees not collected? Is it possible to quantify the fees that should have been charged but weren't? From a sample of monthly transactions, what is the percentage of total fees not charged to customers? What is the amount? How many customers does this represent?

Answering these questions determines how big this problem is and influences the amount of attention management is likely to give. If uncollected fees average less than $15.00 apiece and the monthly total is under $250 in an area whose monthly customer service fees are over $10,000, management may not be greatly concerned. If uncollected fees represent 15% of the area's potential fee revenue, the condition may deserve greater attention.

Analyzing the size of a problem helps build a persuasive presentation. It anticipates the questions and objections a reader is likely to raise, it puts a value on the audit comment and recommendation, and

PERSUASIVE TECHNIQUES

- Describe the conclusion directly and concretely.
- Offer factual evidence.
- Avoid overstating, understating, or misstating the facts.
- Write descriptions of cause rather than symptoms.
- Describe the size of the problem.
    - Number or percentage of exceptions:
        - —Based on sample   —Based on full population
    - $ Value of items with exceptions:
        - —Total   —Average   —Smallest or largest
    - $ Value or volume of the function
        - —Daily, monthly, or annually
- Compare statistics to a meaningful standard.

EXAMPLES

Weak	Persuasive
Few analytical tools have been developed and the branch has not implemented automated applications for the numerous reports, schedules, and documentation being produced manually.	Manual reports now requiring three days per month can be produced in about four hours by automating the reporting.
Of the 20 largest overdrafts open on the audit date, eight had been open an unusually long period of time.	Overdrafts totaling $320,000 and representing 60% of all overdrafts over $5,000 had been open for more than 15 days as of March 1.
Documentation exceptions existed in purchasing.	Fifty-five purchase orders, representing a half-million dollars in merchandise bought, did not list the price.
The amounts of fees for specialized customer services are not consistently collected.	Fifteen percent of total fees due the company have not been collected, and were due more than two months ago.

it positions the point as important for management to know about. From the auditor's perspective, this analysis helps to differentiate between less significant and more material items. Quantification puts problems in perspective for management decision-making.

Comparing statistics to meaningful standards also puts a finding in perspective. For example: "Applications take an average of 39 days to process. Regulation B requires that they be completed in 30." Or: "Overdrafts have been open for up to 20 days, in contrast to the bank's requirement to have them cleared in five." Comparisons to the norm also show the size of a problem. To describe an increase in backlog, an auditor wrote: "January's backlog consisted of 1,250 items. Last year, average monthly backlog was 300 items." Percentage of total items is another meaningful comparison. "January's backlog represents 14% of total volume, as compared to a normal backlog of 3%." You may want to show the degree of change by making a comparison: "Customer complaints increased 75% over last month." These statements, showing a trend or contrasting numbers, are significantly more powerful than ambiguous conclusions such as "Backlog has increased substantially."

In some cases, quantifying a finding will result in the additional benefit of more precisely defining the effect or business significance of the facts you present. For instance, by describing the size of overdrafts, the writer can clarify the amount of exposure or liability: "Overdrafts totaling $320,000 and representing 60% of all overdrafts over $5,000 had been open for more than fifteen days as of March 1. The bank will be liable for this amount if the overdrafts are not resolved." In the case of purchasing: "Fifty-five purchase orders, representing a half-million dollars in merchandise bought, did not list prices."

Remember to apply the summary of persuasive techniques in Exhibit 5-2 to make your comments and recommendations convincing.

Show the Effect from Management's Point of View

To gain acceptance of your point and recommendation, you must address the next question business managers will ask you: "So what?" "What can go wrong as a result of this condition, or what will we gain from acting on this recommendation?" Your comments are valuable to management when they determine an adverse effect on the business or identify a specific benefit.

The effect, whether expressed as a risk or a benefit, must be presented from the perspective of management, not necessarily from that of the auditor. Some managers may perceive audit's view of the effect as too narrow, not focusing on the "bottom line." They may interpret recommendations as being for the benefit of the audit department, not for their own benefit.

Unconvincing presentations result from cliched, vague, or overused statements of risk and benefit. Auditors may describe the effect as: "lack of accountability," "no audit trail," "insufficient documentation," "violation of bank policy," "noncompliance with regulations," or "financial loss or embarrassment." Benefits presented to management may include: "strengthen internal control and accountability," "enhance procedures," "improve documentation," "provide consistency," "ensure separation of duties," or "reduce exposure to financial loss." These may be great audit and control benefits, but they need to be translated to management's language if they are to work as part of your persuasive strategy.

For a persuasive comment, translate the vague and predictable phrases into concrete elements. Avoid cliched statements, which are meaningless and overlooked by your readers. To build your strategy, think through your finding in three terms: features, risks, and benefits. Features describe the conditions, specifying the problem in precise terms. Features help to state the finding clearly, but in themselves are not persuasive elements. Risks define what has gone wrong or could go wrong as a result of the condition. They pinpoint exposures, weaknesses, and disadvantages that managers want to avoid or reduce in their businesses. Benefits define the advantages to be gained by making a change, accepting a recommendation, or eliminating a condition. Risks and benefits are the strategic elements in your writing, moving your report from a factual to a persuasive document. Emphasizing these over features will help you get greater results from your reports.

The outline on the following page illustrates the difference between features, risks, and benefits regarding purchase orders.

Risk may be actual or potential. If the auditors determined that the organization had been overcharged because of lack of pricing, they could identify the exact amount: "Purchasing costs could have been reduced by 15%, or $150,000, over the year." In other cases, the risk will be presented as a potential: "The company could be

---

PURCHASE ORDERS

Features	Risks	Benefits
Price not included	Overcharging	Lowest possible price
		Overall reduction in cost
No bid	Overcharging	Lowest price
	Collusion	Legitimate contractor
	Poor quality of merchandise	Best quality for price

---

overcharged if prices are not fixed at the time the purchase order is issued." Showing perspective by identifying the value of the purchases strengthens the effect, even though it is presented as a potential: "Purchase orders without prices amounted to charges of $35,000 over the last two months."

Another example shows the strengths of considering findings from management's perspective. An auditor's finding was that the consumer loan area was taking an average of 60 days to respond to customers' applications. As a result of this delay, only 25% of the applicants booked their loans with the bank; the rest had already found financing elsewhere. The features of the finding are directly stated and quantified and make a strong case on their own. This was only the auditor's first step, though, in presenting the case to management. She then identified the effects by defining the amount of lost business: "75% of applicants took their consumer loans to other banks because of the 60-day delay in processing loan requests. In January, this represented $1.5 million in lost loan business."

To make a convincing case, the auditor decided to present this less critically and focus instead on the benefits of earlier response to customers. She wrote:

"The consumer lending area can increase their portfolio and interest revenue by responding more quickly to customer applications. The department now takes an average of 60 days

> to respond to loan requests. As a result, in January 75% of the applicants, who requested a total of $1.5 million in financing, had already booked their loans elsewhere by the time the bank responded to their applications."

For complex issues, more research may be needed to identify actual risks and benefits. Instead of simply recommending that management do a cost study to determine the risks, you can gain greater commitment by using an example of one piece of the problem. An auditor used this approach in recommending that automated programs being run under timesharing be moved into production. He felt that one of many advantages in doing this was that it would reduce the need for programmers to submit regularly needed jobs manually. While other parts of this issue required more detailed research to identify the pros and cons, he was able to use the example of manual submission of jobs to make his point about time savings. He quantified the number of regular jobs programmers were submitting monthly and identified that at least five days a month would be saved by moving these jobs to production. This example substantiated the point so that management agreed to continue investigating the feasibility of the recommendation.

Consider every issue you report from the perspective of risk. One audit director emphasizes this approach to his staff by insisting, "If you can't identify the risk, then you don't have a condition to present." Another simply asks her staff "So what?" when they present a comment. Another audit manager refuses to report that an area "is not complying with established procedures." The manager describes that statement as sounding as if it were issued by a compliance officer or rule enforcer. An internal auditor, he says, describes why it is a problem that an area is not following procedures. "What could go wrong? What is the business impact of not following the procedure?" he asks.

Your risk analysis techniques can be valuable tools in writing persuasively. Consider the exposures and risk factors identified in your risk analysis model and determine how your audit comments correspond to those risks. Use the quantitative information contained in your risk model in your reporting. Volume, size, or account balances may be valuable information to help describe exposure.

You may also indicate the level of risk or degree of impact a condition has. For instance, you may describe the level at which a condition has an effect. Is the effect at the level of the branch, the operating unit, the corporation, or the balance sheet? You can also describe the business goal being met by the proposed change. For each comment and recommendation you present, identify which of the following business elements is being addressed: compliance, operational goals, internal control system, productivity, or cost savings.

Overcome Objections

If an opposing argument is strong, you may need to acknowledge and overcome that objection in your report. Often, writers do this indirectly, by anticipating the readers' questions and providing answers in their narratives. Quantification and descriptions of risks and benefits can overcome some forms of resistance before they are verbalized. When your reader's point of view strongly differs from yours, you can counter it by building a balanced argument, recognizing the validity of your reader's opinion, and realistically presenting the pros and cons of your recommendation.

A critical or one-sided approach will further alienate a reader opposed to your recommendation. Show balance and diplomacy by recognizing that other points of view legitimately exist. If a manager insists that it is impossible to process applications in 15 days because of unusual cases requiring more time, acknowledge that position: "While some applications will require up to sixty days for processing, about 75% can be cleared within 15 days." If the need for extra staffing is a legitimate barrier to reducing a backlog, recognize the need: "Additional staffing will be needed temporarily to overcome the backlog, but once the outstanding items are cleared, staffing can return to normal." On other occasions, managers may agree to a compromise and may want both sides of the original proposition acknowledged: "Items over $10,000 should be approved by the manager, even if approval for smaller items is delegated to her assistant."

Balance may involve the recognition of positive accomplishments or efforts even when a problem still exists. For instance: "The unit has already set priorities for the highest-value applications, and these are processed within 30 days. Still, 60% of the applications are on hand for 60 days before notice is sent." Or: "Although management has manual controls for these reports, automation would decrease management's review time and produce greater reliability." "The new system that will eliminate these exposures will not be in use for another year; interim measures will protect the bank from loss during the transition period."

Balance guards against discounting your readers' objections. This recognizes the positive aspects of the opposing points of view without allowing them to deflate your own position. Showing that your recommendation will retain the positive features of the current system or the alternative proposal and include additional benefits as well can create a persuasive, yet balanced argument.

Effective audit reports do much more than present facts and recommendations. They offer convincing evidence of problems and opportunities and include practical, beneficial recommendations for change. Persuasive writers take responsibility for showing the significance of their comments, understanding findings from management's point of view, and analyzing the costs and values of their recommended actions.

The value of your audit report lies in its ability to influence readers to change. You can strengthen your report's effectiveness by quantifying problems, describing the value or volume of operations, identifying risks and exposures, giving practical examples, and anticipating and overcoming readers' objections. Strong writers use these techniques not to produce greater volume in their reports, but to get greater results from their work.

6

Writing Constructively, Not Critically

In face-to-face discussions, we know that our manner of presentation is as important as the substance of our message in influencing our listener's response. A word, tone of voice, or movement of the eye may decide whether a person feels accepting or defensive, criticized or supported, fairly treated or unjustly accused. As much as eighty percent of our message may come through tone of voice and nonverbal behavior. Effectively selecting tone and managing behavior helps an individual reach agreement with and influence others.

In writing, you also convey a tone that readers react to, either positively or negatively. Your message is altered by your emphasis, organization, word choice, and selection of data. As we saw in Chapter 3, you may be strong and forceful, neutral and factual, or suggestive and supportive by changing your emphasis and selection of supporting data. Different persuasive strategies may be effective depending on the significance of the issue you are presenting, the organizational context, and the styles of the managers you are addressing.

To support the persuasive strategy you select, you must continually focus the readers' attention on the substance of your message, not on the language. As you overcome resistance by providing proper support, you must also avoid creating resistance by choosing the wrong word. Arguments have started over a single word in a report. Is the backlog "significant," "substantial," or simply "large?" Time and attention may go into these discussions and detract from identifying a solution to the backlog. Sometimes arguments are not only started but also lost over the choice of a word. Language that makes recipients feel criticized may alienate them and make it impossible for you to reach understanding or agreement.

No matter how significant or minor the issue you are describing, no matter how forceful or indirect you choose to be in your strategy, you can always write constructively—and more persuasively—by applying the following principles.

- Avoid judgmental language and unsupported generalizations.

- State positive ideas in positive language.

- Provide balance and perspective.

- Emphasize benefits, recommendations, and solutions.

Avoid Judgmental Language and Unsupported Generalizations

Audit report writing should be factual and conclusive, not vague and opinionated. While your professional judgment is evident in the conclusions and recommendations you present, your personal opinion should not appear in your report. Although writers are seldom conscious of stating their opinions, their attitudes often show up in words that may sound judgmental or opinionated and, especially if not supported by facts or examples, that are likely to cause defensiveness in your readers.

Use Factual, Concrete Language

Keep your tone constructive by avoiding words that imply or call attention to your opinion. These weaken the argument by positioning the point as a personal evaluation. Notice the effect of the italicized words in the following sentences.

Opinionated Phrases

1. To ensure regulatory compliance and the ability to adapt to pending legislation, *we believe* it is imperative to co-ordinate the compliance function.

2. *We feel* that as the number of accounts increases, the problems with reconciliation will be compounded.

3. Because *we knew* problems would be found, we decided to study the internal processes of this particular office.

4. *Our concern* is that previous attempts to correct this situation have been unsuccessful.

5. *In our opinion,* written procedures should include, at a minimum, the following items.

By removing the opinionated phrases and revising other judgmental language to more objective words, we can make the sentences more constructive.

Nonjudgmental Sentences

1. Coordination of the compliance function is necessary to ensure regulatory compliance and adapt to pending legislation.

2. The difficulty of reconciling will become greater as the number of accounts increases.

3. We selected this office on the basis of its financial performance and staff turnover.

4. This situation has not been corrected even though efforts have been made.

5. Written procedures should include the following items.

Other word choices also convey the writer's opinion of a situation. See how the auditor's point of view comes through in the next examples.

Opinionated Phrases

1. The *appearance* was given *of having inadequate backup* for these two key people. In addition, other staff members *appeared to have plenty of free time, leading us to believe* that delegation of duties is not the norm.

2. Account folders were in *complete disarray,* and *we experienced difficulty even locating them.* Account *officers themselves were uncertain* of where folders were.

3. These recommendations *must* be implemented if management *hopes to* process items on a timely basis.

4. When changes in the original request are made, the department *is forced to redo* the transaction and *must rush* to complete the processing on time.

5. *Excessive* differences indicate a *lack of commitment* to quality goals and expectations.

Any of the above sentences could be dismissed as negative, opinionated, or accusatory. More careful choice of language can make the sentences more appropriate to persuasive report writing.

Nonjudgmental Sentences

1. Duties are not delegated, resulting in little backup for the two key people.

2. Account folders were not organized by account number and were difficult to locate.

3. Acting on these recommendations will help management process items promptly.

4. When changes in the original request are made, the department must redo the transaction, sometimes within the same day to meet deadlines.

5. The unit's 25% difference rate does not meet quality goals.

Some language, in its harshness, seems to sound an alarm or put management under the accusation of wrongdoing. Consider these examples:

Accusatory Tone

1. The rate of change in people, in systems, and in the structure have resulted in a general *deterioration* in the accounting and administrative routine.

2. The *inordinate* number of transactions is putting an *unacceptable* level of stress on controls.

3. The trend is the result of aggressive lending and is *exacerbated* by the heavy work loads and *lack of depth* in the lending staff.

4. The staff *was not prepared to cope* with the volumes of work required, *and management had not been available* to provide the necessary direction.

5. Due to personnel's *inability* to track down supporting documentation, our testing could not be completed.

Watch your language carefully to avoid expressing your judgments and opinions.

Be Aware of Connotations

Pay special attention to the connotations of often used phrases. You may use such terms so automatically that you no longer think about the meanings they convey. The following list identifies words that connote serious or intentional wrongdoing. Readers may hear these as accusations. Use these words sparingly, reserving them for only those few occasions when you want to highlight the seriousness of a problem.

ACCUSATORY CONNOTATIONS

Significant	Failure	Deviations	Discrepancies
Inadequate	Inability	Violations	Deteriorations

Even phrases used to describe audit work and results may have unintentional connotations. "The review *disclosed* significant findings," "We *discovered* these exceptions," and "The investigation *revealed* numerous control weaknesses" imply that you are seeking out and digging up hidden improprieties. "Disclosed," "discovered," and "revealed" are strong verbs, best reserved for investigations of suspected fraud. Phrases such as "we identified" or "we reported" are much less judgmental and express a more objective tone in an audit report. Even the word "findings" may sound negative to some readers.

One writer, ignoring the significance of her words, wrote that her audit objective was "to identify control weaknesses." That certainly got the audit and the report off to a negative start.

A confused or mixed tone can be disorienting to a reader. In the following recommendation, the writer started off with a soft tone and gradually shifted into much more commanding language. "Audit would like to recommend appointing a manager to authorize all purchase orders and to review orders received for accuracy and timeliness. No orders should be sent out and no merchandise shall be received without proper approval. Approval will be given only after a manager verifies price, quantity, and issue date." What starts as a suggestion ("would like to recommend") turns into a mandate ("no merchandise shall be received").

Another report writer made a similar attempt, leading with a positive tone, but ending on a strong negative. "A report of this type is meant to be constructive in nature. Its purpose is to identify areas of weakness in regard to internal controls, and to recommend approaches to improvement. Therefore, the absence of comments of a complimentary nature should not be construed to imply that operations are deficient or unsound."

Avoid Unsupported Generalizations

Vague language often leads to a request for clarification or a defensive rebuttal. Words such as "numerous," "excessive," and "substantial" are imprecise. Readers will want quantification. They may also take a stand against your statement, which they consider judgmental and unsupported. The auditor's and the manager's definitions of "numerous" or "substantial" may differ, and the two may not be able to reach agreement on the point in their battle over the choice of the word. Instead of saying, "A substantial number of orders were processed," choose a more concrete option. Give numbers: "2,500 orders were processed in May." Or provide a comparison: "20% more orders were processed in May than in April." You may also show perspective: "Seventy percent of all departmental orders were processed by this unit in May."

Generalizations are equally dangerous when expressing conclusions and recommendations. "Operations are not functioning properly" is broad and may be given many interpretations. "Transactions need to be posted more timely" could be more concretely stated as "Transactions should be posted on the same day they are received."

State Positive Ideas in Positive Language

Auditors are not in the habit of including many positive statements in their reports, sometimes going to great lengths to avoid saying anything positive. Even when the overall conclusion of the audit is positive, auditors may express that idea in negative language. "No exceptions were noted" is a common example. This is the "generally good, however" syndrome. It recognizes that something positive should be said, but shows a reluctance to come right out and say it. To make your reports more balanced, look for opportunities to include positive statements. This does not mean putting a positive veneer on a negative comment; it means stating positive ideas in positive language. Here are examples of sentences that can be restated positively.

Negative	Positive
None of the items failed to pass the compliance test.	All items were in compliance.
Securities were not left unattended without someone in the area.	Securities were safeguarded.
Let us know if there is a problem responding by Dec. 15.	We look forward to receiving your response by Dec. 15.
We foresee few obstacles to hinder us provided we do not fail to act quickly.	We can accomplish our goals by acting quickly.

Opportunities for positive comments include:

Results of Testing. Many auditors design their communication to management as "exception-only" reporting. This is concise and efficient, but results in negative reports. In every audit, some test results are positive: All items reviewed are completely documented, the staff consistently follows procedures, or all accounts are reconciled daily. Determine the most significant positive results and report these to senior management. Techniques for presenting positive results in the conclusion are described in Chapter 7.

Accomplishments or Efforts That Put a Problem in Perspective. In some cases an error has occurred or a control weakness exists even though management has made a good-faith effort to prevent or correct the problem. Recognizing this effort can build greater cooperation in reaching agreement on action. For example, "The unit has established procedures, but training has not yet been completed and full compliance is not in place."

Provide Balance and Perspective

Keep problems in perspective by recognizing priorities based on goals and risks. Broader business goals may have slowed down implementation of new controls or weakened existing controls. Weigh the two factors. If the exposure or control weakness is greater than the gain made by accomplishing other goals, then you will emphasize the risk and show that the business gain has been made at a larger expense. If, on the other hand, the gain has been greater than the risk created, it may be constructive to report the condition in that light. For instance, "The 40% growth in the number of loans made in the last year has resulted in an increase in missing documentation." Simply reporting the missing documentation could cause managers to believe you are looking at issues out of context.

Managers may think your written statement exaggerates an issue and may ask you to change the wording. Sometimes this happens because you have not provided perspective on the issue. Balancing the positive and negative may help resolve this. "Although the unit keeps data on processing time and accuracy, they do not monitor these figures weekly to evaluate their compliance with quality standards." "Managers confirm these trades by phone, but do not receive a written confirmation from the customer." "Procedures developed in the last year are still in draft form and have not been issued to employees."

Do not exaggerate by itemizing minor points and making them appear larger than they are. If you have given management a list of missing loan documentation, do not repeat that list in your report. Summarize: "We reported missing documentation, and loan officers completed these credit files."

Credit for Action Taken. Follow-up on previous audit recommendations often gives an opportunity for more positive statements. Common summaries of follow-up are: "The majority of the findings from the previous audit were corrected," or "No major problems were noted in the follow-up of previous recommendations."

Using more concrete language can make these statements more positive. For example: "Accountability for revenues was increased by developing a new logging system. A planned renovations program has begun, and a procedures manual has been written for operating personnel."

Remember also to give credit for action taken on items in the current report. For situations that have been corrected, either drop the comment from the final report or describe the action that was taken.

You may also emphasize solutions by giving credit for action already taken. Some auditors write a description of testing they did, problems they found, and—finally—action management took. The following excerpt illustrates this style of writing.

> At the time we tested contract payments, procedures included recording payments in customer files to complement accounts receivable reports. In 50% of the files tested, this information was missing. Because accounts receivable reports are also discarded, we could not be assured that payments and billings were properly reviewed. Since that time, the department developed an integrated data base to record billings and payments. This system provides more efficient records and facilitates appropriate review and problem-solving.

A more results-oriented version of this issue follows.

> The unit developed an integrated data base to record billings and payments, correcting the previous condition of documentation missing from customer files.

Even more constructive are reports that emphasize results and solutions over recommendations. Instead of publishing "finding-recommendation-response" to senior management, these forward-looking reports include actions or solutions. After reaching agreement with management, the solution is included in the report and the recommendation is deleted.

89

Emphasize Benefits, Recommendations, and Solutions

Two of the most frequently used words in audit reports, "not" and "should," create a reprimanding tone. Replacing these words with "can" and "will" gives a more constructive, results-oriented description of the point you are presenting. Here is an example of the transformation.

> *Original Wording:* "Many transfers for items returned have only one line item recorded. In several cases, we noted situations where a department prepared multiple transfers in one day and did not consolidate these. To improve efficiency, transfers should be consolidated."

> *Revised Wording:* "Transfers of one item can be consolidated onto a single form to reduce paper." Or, "Consolidating multiple transfers of single items onto one form will reduce paper and time."

Instead of citing a problem using negative language followed by a standard audit recommendation, the revised report presents a potential solution and identifies a benefit. This is a more constructive approach to presenting an operational recommendation.

You can alter the tone of your writing by deciding whether to describe the risk of a current condition or the benefit of a proposed solution. Here is a negative statement of risk:

> No control exists to independently check the accuracy and completeness of inventory records. Errors could go undetected, or inventory could be removed from the stockroom without it being recorded.

By changing the focus to a proposed solution and its benefit, you can make the language more positive:

> Separating record keeping from other stockroom duties will ensure that all inventory movement is properly entered into the perpetual system. Independent balancing and reconciliation verify that all entries are complete and accurate.

90

Your decision on emphasis—whether to stress problems or benefits—depends on your understanding of your readers, their objections, and their sensitivities. Be careful not to offend or alienate and lose the opportunity for managers to be receptive to your recommendations. One report writer almost did just that when he wrote a report in a harsh, critical tone. All issues were presented in this style: "It appears that the number of installations and removals of equipment may be excessive and not cost-justified." The writer explained that he used this ambiguous language because management already knew they had a problem with budget overruns. He said management had requested this audit as a way to help solve the problem. In that case, his tone was wrong. Thinking about his audience and objectives, he rewrote the report to stress solutions and benefits, not to restate already known issues to management. Here is an example of one of the revised statements: "The cost of equipment installations and removals can be reduced by using a form analyzing costs and alternatives for discretionary cases."

Constructive, nonjudgmental language is necessary in persuasive writing. Your careful choice of wording and your avoidance of negative cliches will make your report more factual, professional, and acceptable to management.

Remember to give credit where credit is due, take advantage of opportunities for positive language, and offer a fair balance of positive and negative. Focus on solutions, results, and benefits; do not dwell on problems alone. These writing techniques will help you build on your collaborative relationship with management and will lead your organization to more constructive results from your audit reports.

PRESENTING TO SENIOR MANAGEMENT

7

Writing the
Audit Conclusion

In their best-selling book, *In Search of Excellence,* Thomas Peters and Robert Waterman quote B. Charles Ames, past president of Reliance Electric:

> I can get a division manager to cough up a seventy-page proposal overnight. What I don't seem to be able to do is get a one-page analysis, a graph, say, that shows the trend and projection, and then says, 'Here are the three reasons it might be better; here are the three things that might make it worse.'

The direct, analytical, succinct style of writing Mr. Ames calls for is what your senior management expects from your reports. Effective audit reports offer more than a list of comments, findings, or exceptions. They explain the significance of audit results and answer the questions of a senior-management audience:

- How significant are these points within the organization?

- What's the overall condition of the area? Should I be worried? Reassured?

- What is the value of acting on the audit recommendations? What is being done now to maintain good operations or improve weak ones?

You can answer these questions and contribute to management's decision-making by writing a balanced, concrete, and succinct conclusion, or opinion, for each of your audit reports.

What Management Gains from the Conclusion

A well-written conclusion gives management the information, perspective, and balance they need for decision- making.

By highlighting your major comments and offering your judgment of their significance, you can help management evaluate audit results and decide on appropriate action. Rather than turning over a list of problems, you can show management where the problems—and accomplishments—fit within the overall performance of the unit and the organization.

In the conclusion, you can also describe the business implications of the audit results. Turning your attention to an executive-level audience, you should consider the audit points from their perspective, describing specific consequences—risk or exposure—or contributions of the area's performance.

Finally, the conclusion offers a vehicle for constructive commentary and solutions. Too often, a standard audit report format allows little space for positive remarks. A conclusion is balanced, describing positive as well as negative results.

Why, Then, the Reluctance to Write a Conclusion?

Only 67% of bank internal audit departments include a conclusion or opinion in their reports,* and the professional standards (The Institute of Internal Auditors) suggest but do not require that reports include this section.

Why the reluctance? Audit managers say the conclusion requires language that is "too committed," that line management may object to the wording, or that management will not read the body of the report if a paragraph of conclusion is on the first page.

With these fears in mind many auditors choose to avoid writing a conclusion. Others do so reluctantly, spending little time and effort on this section. They may go to one of two extremes, writing a brief, general narrative or presenting a list of all comments and recommendations in the report.

These writers overlook a powerful source of influence in their reports. By writing a well-developed conclusion, you can avoid the arguments over language, get your readers' attention, and draw them into the body of your report.

*BAI 1988 Survey of Bank Audit Practices.

Common Styles of the Audit Conclusion

First, we shall evaluate two representative styles of the audit conclusion.

> EXAMPLE 1:
>
> Based on our review, it was felt that generally these systems are well-controlled and are functioning properly. However, there are some areas where weaknesses exist that will require your attention. These items are discussed in the attached report.
>
> EXAMPLE 2:
>
> Compliance with corporate travel policies and procedures appeared to be good. Travel on bank vehicles for personal use, however, was not being reported on a consistent basis. Controls for detecting errors in calculating personal and business fares were not adequate. Also, the delegation of authority for an individual to approve the use of company vehicles was not documented. These and other items are detailed in the Findings section of this report.

These samples represent two common styles of the audit conclusion. Example 1 is the *boilerplate*. It is so broad and its language so vague that it can be used in any audit report. You can pull this directly from your word processor into the report without having to change a single word.

While terms such as "well-controlled," "functioning properly," and "areas of weakness" are useful for broad summaries, they are not specific enough to stand on their own. Without support or examples, they are meaningless in the conclusion. The purpose of the conclusion is to express a clear message to management, but in Example 1 we have little more than filler.

Example 2 is much more specific and gives particular examples of audit comments included in the report. Still, the message is confusing. The first sentence, containing the overall opinion, is positive. The second sentence shifts tone and direction, beginning with the telltale word "however," and turns the rest of this paragraph to negative comments.

This *generally good, however*... style is an unbalanced construction that often leaves readers puzzled, wondering how the condition can be good when the summary highlights only negative findings and five pages of problem areas follow.

Conclusions need to be more precise, concrete, and balanced than the preceding samples if they are to be effective executive summaries.

Six Steps to an Effective Conclusion

To write an attention-getting and effective conclusion, you can take the following steps:

- Answer the audit objective(s).

- Choose concrete supporting information.

- Use an appropriate and consistent tone.

- Balance the positive and negative.

- Offer perspective.

- Comment on management's response.

Answer the Audit Objective

The conclusion, like the condition statement for an individual comment, should answer the objective addressed by the audit work.

When you begin to write your conclusion, answer the objective directly. Avoid statements such as "The condition of the area was generally good," or "Controls were generally satisfactory." Make your conclusion specific. For example, consider the audit objective: "To determine the accuracy of account balances and evaluate the adequacy of control over input procedures." A conclusion might be: "Account balances were accurate, and controls over input procedures were adequate."

When the audit includes multiple objectives, be sure to address each of them in the conclusion.

EXAMPLE:

Audit Objective: Determine if staffing in the credit card area is sufficient, if management is achieving plans for business growth and profitability, and if controls over the processing of payments are adequate.

> *Conclusion:* While management has achieved targets for growth and profitability and maintained sufficient staffing levels, processing controls over credit card payments are insufficient.

When you have a series of objectives for the audit, it may sometimes be appropriate to answer each objective in a separate sentence. Here is an example:

> The financial and accounting controls were effective to ensure that the fund was properly administered and safeguarded. Advances and expenditures from the fund were properly authorized and in accordance with company requirements. Controls over special transactions were effective to ensure that funds and property held for evidence were properly accounted for and maintained.

To make for easier reading in a long list of conclusions, the writer could format the narrative by presenting each point as a bulleted item or in numerical sequence.

> 1. Financial and accounting controls were effective to ensure that the fund was properly administered and safeguarded.
>
> 2. Advances and expenditures were properly authorized and in accordance with company requirements.
>
> 3. Controls over special transactions were effective to ensure that funds and property held for evidence were properly accounted for and maintained.

In even more comprehensive audits, the conclusion may be broken down into sections. You might, for instance, write a separate paragraph for each of the major sections of an audit, such as financial, operational, and compliance. With that structure, you would have room for developing each part of the conclusion separately, offering examples and providing appropriate supporting information.

Answering the audit objective is the foundation to building a good conclusion. As we will see in later examples, starting with this technique can also help you establish appropriate balance.

Choose Concrete Supporting Information

From the general opening statement of your conclusion, you must move to more concrete supporting information. As in any persuasive narrative, you need to support your opinion with facts, examples, comparisons, or other data that will help prove your point. Executives reading the conclusion should understand and be able to visualize the meaning of your results. Choose examples that create a picture of the audited unit.

The first tool for a persuasive conclusion is clear language. Choose words that are concrete and specific. Avoid words with multiple definitions or connotations. In Example 1, the writer used phrases such as "functioning properly" and "some areas where weaknesses exist that will require your attention." Both of these phrases are ambiguous. In what way are the systems functioning properly? Does this mean that payments are being processed promptly, or that transactions are valid and proper? Define general terms so that they are specific to the area you are describing. Instead of writing "some areas of weakness," cite the particular weaknesses. Make your words so clear that they cannot be misinterpreted.

The following is an example of a conclusion offering only generalizations.

> "The audit revealed *control and procedural weaknesses* that should be addressed by management. *Many of these problems* were noted in a previous audit of the area. In our opinion, *the following exceptions* present *significant risk and liability* to the company's assets and customer base."

The italicized terms in this conclusion are examples of words to avoid in your writing. Wherever possible, use concrete substitutes for these general phrases. If you do use these words, follow up with specific examples.

Avoid the following terms in your conclusion, or include specific examples.

Buzzwords

Generally improved

Some control deficiencies

Recommendations for improvement

100

The following exceptions

Some weaknesses

Potential for loss

Lack of internal control

Areas requiring attention

Need for some improvement

Need to strengthen procedures

The implementation of recommendations

Compromise integrity

Tighten controls

Vague and Concrete Conclusions

Vague:
Physical security weaknesses were noted in the area.

Concrete:
Physical control of computer equipment and sensitive information was not adequate. The area needed surveillance cameras and more restricted access policies to prevent unauthorized individuals from entering the data processing area.

Vague:
In our opinion, the area was well-controlled.

Concrete:
Operations were well-controlled. Accounts were in balance and compliance with established policies and control requirements was good. Management had implemented the procedural changes made necessary by Regulation XXX, and the processing backlog had been reduced to 200 items from the 450 of last year.

Concrete writing requires confident writing. Specific words and concrete language represent clear, conclusive thoughts. Be careful not to weaken your message by using qualifiers. Here is an example of a conclusion with too many qualifiers:

> It appears that existing internal controls in some areas within the scope of this audit do not provide reasonable assurance that the accounting records can be relied on as being accurate.

Qualifying or limiting your opinion causes your writing to lose its impact. In the above sentence, the question still remains: "Are controls adequate or not?" To write strong, concrete conclusions, avoid qualifiers such as the following:

Audit Qualifiers

In our opinion	Generally
It appears that	It is felt that
Based on the review	Within the scope of this audit
Reasonable assurance	Management should consider
May (not) be	

You can lessen the temptation to include qualifiers by consistently applying the first two steps in writing the audit conclusion: answering the objective, and choosing concrete supporting information. Using an objective and factual opening will help you avoid the more judgmental phrases ("well-controlled," "satisfactory," "acceptable") that often cry out for qualifiers.

Use an Appropriate and Consistent Tone

The conclusion reflects the overall tone of your audit report and your opinion on the condition of the area. In writing the conclusion, you must choose and support one tone consistently. For example, your opinion may be positive—controls are adequate and problems identified are minor—or negative—controls are inadequate. In other cases, your opinion will be balanced: Some control objectives are well met, but others are not. Your conclusion must convey one of these three tones unequivocally.

Confusion or misstatement can occur if you are not precise in your construction and choice of words.

Unbalanced constructions are a common cause of confusing tone. The *generally good, however.....* style of conclusion showed an unbalanced construction. This narrative, presenting one positive sentence and four negative sentences, gives the reader conflicting messages. Readers' differing reactions to such unbalanced conclusions are proof of the confusing messages conveyed by these narratives. Consider the following paragraph:

> **Conclusion**
>
> The results of our review indicated the condition of operations to be good. However, we found several areas that need attention. Efforts need to be intensified to effect reconcilement of several open accounts. In payments processing, testing of automated equipment should be implemented and supervisory observation improved. Also, suspense accounts need attention.

When asked to describe the tone of the above conclusion, some readers say it is positive; others say it is negative. Few describe it as balanced. Whatever tone the writer wanted to convey, it does not come across consistently to all readers.

Inappropriate word choice also contributes to an inconsistent tone. In the example above, the writer suggests that "efforts need to be *intensified*," perhaps using an overly strong verb directly after the statement that operations are good. The contrast in tone is jarring.

In another conclusion, the writer chooses exaggerated words that are likely to leave the reader disoriented.

> Although we found the payroll system to be encumbered by excessive manual processing and lacking in some security measures, it appears to be well-controlled and functioning accurately.

It requires a stretch of the imagination to envision how a system "encumbered with excessive manual processing" can be "well-controlled."

It is essential that all readers receive the same clear and consistent message from the conclusion. When the opinion is strongly positive or negative, that message is not too difficult to convey. When the opinion is balanced, writing an accurate conclusion requires mastery of specific writing techniques.

Balance the Positive and Negative

To balance the scales of positive and negative, the weight must be equal on both sides. If you have some positive results and some negative results from your audit, distribute that weight as you write your conclusion. Many writers load up the negative side of their conclusions, giving only a few words to the positive. That approach tips the scales unmercifully, as we saw in the two examples of the *generally good, however .....* style.

Give weight to both the positive and the negative by offering support for each side. Give examples of positive results. Here are illustrations:

> Operations were well-controlled. Customer account balances were correctly calculated, and penalties were properly assessed.
>
> Revenue was properly collected, deposited, and reported. Expenses were reasonable and proper, and the statement of account fairly presented the financial condition for the period audited.
>
> The department has developed programs to improve the quality of operations. These include: redesign of workflow, monitoring of production statistics, and development of quality standards.

Once you have identified the positive supporting examples, you can begin to balance them appropriately with your recommendations. You will need to emphasize your most important ideas by positioning your content correctly and establishing the right proportions.

Your most important ideas should occupy prominent positions within the section as a whole and the individual sentences. Within the conclusion, put the idea you want to emphasize in the first paragraph.

> SAMPLE CONCLUSION
> **Emphasis on the Positive**
>
> The department's controls were adequate to ensure correct

customer balances and the proper and timely collection of fees and penalties. Controls remained sufficient throughout the many policy and personnel changes of the last year.

Certain operating procedures required improvement. Adjustment authorizations were not consistently complete and accurately documented. Also, an outdated operating manual, while not causing significant errors, was slowing down the training of new staff.

SAMPLE CONCLUSION
Emphasis on the Negative

Operating procedures required improvement. Adjustment authorizations were not consistently complete and accurately documented. Also, an outdated operating manual was slowing down the training of new staff.

Controls were adequate to ensure correct customer balances and the proper and timely collection of fees and penalties.

Besides repositioning the paragraphs, the writer has also varied the proportion of space given to the positive and negative in these two examples. In the first conclusion, the writer gives more positive support; in the second, the writer includes more examples of weaknesses.

Another balancing technique is the positioning of ideas within sentences. Ideas are emphasized when they appear in a sentence's independent clause; they become de-emphasized when they appear in a dependent clause.

Consider this sentence from the more positive conclusion above: "An outdated operating manual, while not causing significant errors, was slowing down the training of new staff."

The more important idea, placed in the independent clause, is "slowing down the training."

Now consider another version of the sentence: "While the outdated operating manual was slowing down the training of new staff, it was not causing significant errors."

The emphasis now is on "not causing significant errors," and the sentence has a more positive tone.

The writer could give equal weight to the two ideas in the sentence by placing them in similarly constructed clauses: "An outdated operating manual was slowing down the training of new staff, but it was not causing significant errors."

Main Idea   **Subordinate Idea**
_____   _____

Independent Clause   Dependent Clause

       Balanced Ideas (Both of Equal Importance)

Independent Clause   Independent Clause
_____   _____

Unbalanced Construction   **Balanced Construction**

Positive opinion	Summary statement of conclusion
. . . However . . .	Positive conclusion with examples
Negative findings	Negative conclusion with examples or effects

---

Offer Perspective

Taken out of context, audit results may be difficult for readers unfamiliar with the area to interpret. A list of recommendations, or problems, may not offer much help in interpreting audit results. Executive management may still want to know: How big are the problem areas? What are the implications of these points within the organization? How will problems be fixed? Are the operations particularly strong or weak?

You can provide perspective by describing the significance or effect of the major audit points, including meaningful comparisons, and by identifying underlying causes.

106

As in the detailed audit comments, a description of effect or significance can clarify an otherwise ambiguous point. Sometimes, you need to show the extent of a problem, explaining just how widespread it is or how far its implications may reach. In the following example, the writer illustrated the extent of a weakness by describing potential negative effects and at the same time showing the limitations of the problem.

> Although we have made recommendations to improve operations and administration of the data base, the weaknesses mentioned will not jeopardize the security of the processing environment.

Another conclusion focuses on the effects of the underlying problem:

> A system for acquiring, controlling, and using company vehicles has been established, but the procedures are not generally followed. This has resulted in the purchase of cars without a cost analysis, inaccurate mileage information in the Auto Management System, and the unauthorized use of bank cars.

In another conclusion, the writer gives concrete examples of the effect:

> A weakness in compiling financial data resulted in misstated financial statements. The cash account was understated by $28,000, and the loan loss reserve account showed a debit balance of $100,000.

As in the example above, quantification of the significance can be valuable. If the most significant comments in the body of the report quantify the risk, loss, or cost savings, present that information in the conclusion.

Comparisons may also put results into perspective. You can show whether the area's performance is better or worse than it was at the time of the last audit by commenting on action taken on prior audit recommendations, changes in the quality of operations, performance trends, or unusual circumstances that influence the interpretation of results.

In the sample conclusion on page 99, the writer provides perspective by describing unusual circumstances: "Controls remained sufficient throughout the many policy and personnel changes of the last year."

In the next example, the writer mentions improvements since the last audit.

Overall, internal control has improved since the last audit. Documentation is more complete, and reports to customers are accurate.

Examples of trends may also be useful: "Last year, processing delays averaged 30 days; this year, those delays have grown to an average of 50 days."

Finally, itemized exceptions may be tied together and made more meaningful by identifying their underlying cause.

Processing delays, data-entry errors, and incomplete documentation resulted from high turnover (70% in the last year) and lack of training.

Descriptions of effect, comparisons, and identification of causes all contribute to a stronger, more analytical conclusion.

Comment on Management's Response

While audit results and their interpretation form the body of the conclusion, the good writer will not stop there. It is management's corrective action that results in value to the organization, and that positive step may be an effective closing item for the audit conclusion.

Some conclusions make a general reference to management's response:

Management has begun to correct the weaknesses identified in the report.

Management accepted our recommendations and agreed to make appropriate changes.

Action is underway to implement the required changes described in the report.

108

If you use your conclusion as a summary report to the Audit Committee, it is especially important to comment on management action. Each overall conclusion may be followed by a description of the action. For example:

> Processing delays, data-entry errors, and incomplete documentation resulted from high turnover (70% in the last year) and lack of training. Management has begun a training and quality- control program that has already decreased delays and is expected to reduce errors within the next month.

Other reports include a more detailed statement, often with a heading such as "Action Steps," listing the solutions to problems identified in the report.

The effective closing to an audit conclusion looks forward, describing solutions and positive actions and it answers management's final questions by describing what is being or will be done.

Summary

A conclusion adds great value to the information you present to senior management. A direct, analytical, and interpretive synthesis pinpoints the essential meaning of your results and shows the significance of the audit comments. A balanced and concrete conclusion lets your organization's executives visualize the condition of the audited unit and understand whether appropriate action is being taken to maintain or improve quality. By avoiding the *boilerplate* and *generally good, however......* styles, you can give management the analysis needed to make informed decisions.

8

Organizing and Formatting the Audit Report

A well-designed audit report will catch your readers' attention, invite them to browse through or read the content, and meet the needs of readers at various levels in your organization. The appearance and structure of your report will work for you and your audience if you apply the following techniques.

- Include the appropriate sections.

- Write a summary of results.

- Layer the report for multiple audiences.

- Format the report for easy reading.

Include the Appropriate Sections

Internal audit reports may include some or all of the following sections:

- Audit objective.
- Scope.
- Background information.
- Audit opinion or conclusion.
- Summary.
- Results of work.
- Appendices.

The Institute of Internal Auditors' Statement on "Communicating Results" requires the objective, scope, and results of work in each audit report. Other parts should be included if they help your readers understand and accept your results or act on your recommendations.

Audit Objective and Scope

The objective and scope, sometimes combined into one statement of "Purpose" or "Introduction," explain the framework of your audit. This information clarifies the subject and the extent of your work. It helps set the readers' expectations for the content of the report and allows them to put your results into perspective.

The objective consists of: 1) the action or performance, 2) the subject, and 3) the purpose. For example,

> "Verify the accuracy of account balances."

> "Determine if assets are properly safeguarded."

> "Evaluate the adequacy of backup procedures."

> "Test the completeness of documentation."

Some audits may have one general statement of objective, such as "Evaluate the adequacy of internal controls." Others may have several more specific objectives to define the work done. The more clearly stated the objective, the more structured and informative your results and opinion will be.

The scope identifies the extent of work done within the audited unit. This section may include:

- Sections of an operation included in audit coverage. An audit of Human Resources may focus on benefits, payroll, and EEO compliance, but not include training or employee relations.

- Sample size and criteria. For example: "We reviewed 40 of the 134 loans in the portfolio. This included all loans over $1 million, and at least five loans from each of the unit's lending officers." Or: "We tested 50 invoices, totaling over $300,000, paid during June."

- Time frame covered.

- Parts of the operation excluded from audit coverage.

112

The scope does not itemize audit procedures or steps. Line management will know the detailed scope from your initial planning meetings and will have the chance to clarify questions on the extent of work in your closing conferences. Senior managers rarely need that level of detail, as they are reading the report to learn your results, not to judge the sufficiency of your work. If certain managers want more detail on audit testing, include that in an appendix.

The objective and scope give the reader a framework to understand the content of your report. This section should highlight only the information your readers need to make sense of your conclusions. Allow the report to emphasize results and recommendations by keeping your introductory section brief and leading your readers into the body of your report as quickly as possible.

Background Information

A background section gives a management overview of the area audited. This description may be valuable when the unit is new, complex, or unique or when your audience includes readers unfamiliar with the unit. Background information is not necessary if you are reporting on areas well-known to your management.

Think of the background section as a description of a business unit, and consider portraying the area in some of the following terms:

- Function or purpose.

- Size or volume.

- Profits, expenses, or other business contribution.

- Major services and products.

- Structure or organization.

- Recent changes.

- Unknown or unusual terms.

These items show management the significance of the area, highlight exposures or risks in the operation, and clarify understanding.

As you select material for background information, avoid lists of operating procedures, forms, and reports. The purpose of this section is to give a business overview, not to educate readers in the detailed workings of an area. Operational descriptions will not be necessary if you write the body of your report simply and directly and avoid extensive use of jargon and technical language.

113

Avoid dumping extraneous information into this section. Apply two criteria to every piece of information you consider presenting: Do the readers need to know this? and Do they want to know this? The following excerpt from a section on background information includes more detail than readers need or want.

> Generally Accepted Accounting Principles require the company to properly recognize expenses for goods and services in the period they are received. For this purpose, the General Manager-Accounting issues an annual letter and set of instructions to all districts regarding year- end accruals. The instructions require accruals to be prepared covering materials and services actually received or which the company has taken title of, for which vendor billing will not be received and paid by year- end. This also includes any employee reimbursements applicable to the year under report. The procedures further require that all accrual information be submitted to the Accounting Office on Form 22GDC, Request for Monthly Accrual, and be approved by division level or higher. The total company year-end accrual for 19xx was $55,258,000.

The detailed outlining of procedures is unnecessary. All the reader needs to know is the purpose of accruals and the yearly total. Revising this excerpt to highlight the key information helps achieve another objective of a background information section. That objective is to help readers interpret the significance of results presented in the report. Size, volume, profits, or value are useful elements to meet this need. The background on accruals, for example, might be condensed to this:

> At year-end, accruals must be done for all goods and services received or taken title of but not yet paid for. These accruals are necessary to properly record expenses in the period in which they are incurred. Total year-end accruals for 19xx were $55,258,000.

Exhibit 8-1 gives an example of a brief background section that defines terms and describes the size of the operation.

Attachments and Exhibits

Attachments present details necessary to support conclusions or generalizations offered in the report. Separating the detail from the body will help you keep the interest of high-level readers yet still meet the needs of those who require the specific supporting data. Information commonly presented in appendices includes:

- Audit tests or procedures.

- Detailed exceptions.

- Summary graphs or charts of findings.

Attachments must always be appropriately referenced within the report. State the conclusion, then refer to the supporting detail. For example, "Documentation of insurance and collateral was missing from 25% of the loans in four branches. Attachment One shows the number of exceptions in each office." Be sure the attachment is properly labeled to correspond to the initial reference.

Information most appropriate for separation from the body of the report includes detail already presented to line management or data not crucial to proving your conclusion but containing items of interest or significance to senior management. Exhibit 8-2 at the end of this chapter shows detail presented in an attachment to the report.

Write a Summary of Results

If your report is five or more pages long, a summary of results will be valuable for senior management. The summary lets readers skim the report while still learning the significant points you are presenting. Major newspapers such as The Wall Street Journal and The New York Times include news digests to accommodate busy, demanding readers. Adding this touch to your report will also generate greater response from more readers.

A summary may highlight the major comments in a long report or it may give a quick overview of all comments. You may format this section as a brief narrative, a list, or a table of contents.

For short reports, you may want to write one or two paragraphs summarizing the content. An even quicker way of producing a summary is to list the titles of the audit comments or the key phrases of the recommendations as numbered or bulleted items. These should be presented in the same order and in the same words as they appear in the report. "The summary of recommendations" in Exhibit 8-3 illustrates how you can easily use bulleted items as an overview of the report content. Writing this type of summary is quick, as you can use the heading or the first sentence of each comment to compose the outline. This same outline can even be used as a table of contents, as shown in Exhibit 8-4.

Keep in mind that the summary is not the same as the conclusion. The conclusion, as described in Chapter 7, answers the audit objectives, interprets the audit results, and puts them in perspective. The summary is simply an overview of the report content. The sample introduction in Exhibit 8-3 shows the differences between the conclusion and the summary and illustrates how the two sections complement each other. This arrangement—with objective, conclusion, and summary as the introduction—also creates an executive summary that can easily be separated from the body of the report.

Another format for an executive summary is a three-sentence summary of each of the major comments in the report. By pulling the condition, effect, and management action from the body, you can create a succinct summary for executive readers.

Layer the Report for Multiple Audiences

A challenge in writing audit reports is meeting the different needs of many levels of management. While line management may want the detail of all comments, senior executives want a short, crisp report, one that offers a lot of information in a very small space. Balancing these demands calls for a flexible report structure, allowing each reader to find the information of greatest interest to him or her quickly and easily.

Rather than issuing several versions of the same report, you can layer the report so that the highest-level readers have their needs met in the first pages. The rest of the report can build to greater detail.

A layering sequence that lets you address senior management up front follows:

- Cover sheet.

- Table of contents (optional).

- Objective.

- Scope.

- Conclusion.

- Summary of results.

- Results of work.

  (Audit comments and recommendations.)

- Background information.

- Detailed scope (if needed).

- Appendices or exhibits.

Organizing the report this way will put the objective, scope, and conclusion on the first page. This sheet, which may even be separated from the body of the report for distribution to senior management, can become your executive summary. Followed by the summary of results, this page provides the succinct, conclusive overview desired by your top managers and board members. Exhibit 8-3 illustrates how the introduction section of a report can stand on its own for presentation to senior management, and Exhibit 8-5 outlines a report presenting background and scope as attachments.

Arranging the Results of Work Section

In keeping with the principles applied in constructing every other part of the audit report, the results of work section should be arranged with the most important information first. While there are many other logical ways of organizing comments, the direct method will attract the most attention and will be most fitting for your audience. The heading, topic sentence, and recommendation of your first audit comment should present information of immediate and direct significance to management.

To effectively organize this detailed section and hold your readers' interest throughout, you can begin by reviewing all comments and recommendations you intend to include in the report. Go through your pages of results and evaluate them by asking the following questions:

- Are some of the comments related by a common theme: cause, risk, or solution?

- If so, should any of these be consolidated or positioned back-to-back?

- Is there repetition of information or key phrases from one comment to another? If so, combine the similar items or eliminate the repetition.

- Are the most significant items presented in direct, attention-getting language?

- Are headings concrete, concise, and informative?

- Is the amount of detail appropriate? Should any be deleted or moved to appendices?

In a longer audit report, it may be necessary to break down the results of work by section or unit. A Human Resources audit covering several major sections, for example, may be divided according to payroll, benefits, and EEO compliance. A report on a lending area may be organized according to loan quality, documentation, and administration. Subsections like these can help senior management find information quickly in the report and can aid line managers in responding to their areas of responsibility.

When you divide results of work into parts, arrange the parts according to the same principles of direct organization. Within each section, put the most important comment first. Then organize the subsections on the basis of significance.

Format the Report for Easy Reading

Your report must look official, professional, and inviting. A sloppy appearance may suggest sloppy work. Begin with distinctive audit stationery or a cover sheet that identifies your report instantly. Make it stand out from other documents in your managers' in-boxes.

Give an inviting look to the body of the report by making it easy to follow and comfortable to absorb. Pages of straight type, with few breaks and little white space, look forbidding to many readers. Use headings that guide readers through the content and formatting that keeps their eyes moving along the pages. Formatting tools to keep in mind include:

- Headings
  - —Centered headings for major sections
  - —Side headings for subsections individual comments
  - —Boldface type
  - —Underlining

- Bullets and numbers
  - —Listing of items in a series
  - —Indented from side margin

- White Space
  - —Page breaks for new sections
  - —Two to four blank lines between subsections or comments
  - —Ample margins

- Tables or charts
  - —Detailed information
  - —Numerical data

Properly formatted, your report will flow smoothly from page to page and guide the reader from one section to another. A reader will be able to skim the report, learning your major ideas and missing none of your important points.

Use the quality checklist in Exhibit 8-6 to evaluate your own reports. By choosing the appropriate sections, writing a summary, and layering and formatting your content, you will create an informative, interesting, and inviting report that your executives will want to read.

(Exhibits follow)

EXHIBIT 8-1

Sample: Background Information

Personal Trust Administration handles over 2,500 trust and agency accounts with assets of $4 billion. Personal Trust accounts are governed by 12 CFR 9 and are administered by two units: Custody and Probate.

Personal Trust Custody administers personal trust custody, safekeeping, and limited agency accounts. This unit is responsible for the timely and accurate execution of trades, transfers, and other instructions from customers.

Personal Trust Probate administers Executor, Guardian, and Administrator accounts.

EXHIBIT 8-2

Sample: Attachment

Attachment 1

Detail of Differences Between
Subsidiary Accounts and the General Ledger

Account Number	Account Name	Difference
11111	Construction-Commercial	$40,000
22222	Construction-Personal	10,250
33333	Conventional Mortgage	(79,500)
44444	Residential Participation	(83,000)
Net Difference		(122,250)

EXHIBIT 8-3

Sample: Report Introduction and Executive Summary

AUDIT OF CENTRAL CITY BANKING OFFICE
February 20 - March 10, 19xx

AUDIT OBJECTIVES

Our objectives in auditing the Central City Office were to evaluate:

- Adequacy of controls over funds transfer.
- Proper management of investment accounts.
- Compliance with regulations.
- Adequacy of practices for personal and commercial lending and compliance with bank policies.
- Physical controls and safeguarding of cash and valuables.
- Efficiency of operations.

CONCLUSION

Customer authorization was not documented for all funds transfers, and employees' accountability for these transactions was not consistently recorded. Overdrafts in investment accounts were not cleared promptly, and customers were not notified of credit decisions within 30 days, as required by Regulation B. Management has obtained funds-transfer agreements for all commercial customers and established full compliance with policy. Overdrafts are now cleared within five days, and a system has been established to monitor and follow-up on credit applications.

Physical controls and safeguarding of valuables were appropriate, operations were well-managed, and compliance with regulations other than B was satisfactory.

SUMMARY OF RECOMMENDATIONS

- Require written authorization for funds transfer.
- Document employees' authority to transfer funds.
- Manage investment account activity.
- Notify customers of credit decisions promptly.
- Establish policy for nonaccrual loans.
- Improve accuracy of expense reporting.

EXHIBIT 8-4

Sample: Index or Table of Contents

INDEX

LOAN DOCUMENTATION

Maintain Complete Loan Documentation	1
Develop Standards for Timely Review of Documentation	1
Obtain Documents Before Advancing Funds	2
Obtain Evidence of Hazard Insurance	2

COLLATERAL

Improve Control Over Safekeeping of Collateral	3
Revise Procedures for Releasing Collateral	4

OTHER

Reconcile Accrued Interest Receivable Records with the General Ledger Daily	5

EXHIBIT 8-5

Sample: Table of Contents

AUDIT COMMENTS

Wire Transfers	3
Inactive General Ledger Accounts	4
Management Review of Overdraft Activity Reports	5
Account Openings and Signature Cards	6
Attachment A: Audit Scope	7
Attachment B: Background Information	8

EXHIBIT 8-6

Quality Checklist for Audit Reports

1. _____ Are the appropriate sections included?

2. _____ Is there a summary?

3. _____ Does the outline of the report give the reader a quick overview
of the content?

4. _____ Are enough headings used to guide the reader?

5. _____ Are titles written in a consistent style?

6. _____ Is the format inviting?

7. _____ Are the most important comments presented first?

8. _____ Are related comments combined?

9. _____ Is repetition avoided?

10. _____ Is detail presented in exhibits or appendices?

9

Presenting Results to Management and the Audit Committee

Audit reporting keeps managers at many levels in the organization informed of the effectiveness of controls and of strengths and weaknesses throughout the operation. Because the purpose of conveying the information is to initiate change, it is best presented in stages—first to line management so that they can take action, then to senior management to keep them informed and gain their commitment to planned changes, and finally to the Audit Committee to keep them aware of control activities and allow them to fulfill their oversight responsibility.

Since the purpose of reporting to each of these levels is different, the amount of information and the format you will use to present it will vary at each step. To make the reporting process efficient and to avoid the production of several reports for each audit, you can structure a writing and reporting sequence using different components of the same report content and format for each audience. The major steps in the sequence include:

- Oral presentation to line management,
- Written report to line management,
- Report to senior management, and
- Report to the Audit Committee.

Oral Presentation to Line Management

Line managers need to be kept informed of audit results throughout the fieldwork. The purpose of this ongoing communication is to get agreement on the facts, correct any errors or problems identified by audit testing, and initiate agreement on future actions. This face-to-face communication process will offer more detail than any of the other reporting phases. If you have identified missing documentation, you will give a copy of your worksheet to management immediately so that they can confirm your facts, locate unfiled documents, and begin to collect the required forms. If few documents are missing and you are assured that this problem does not occur frequently, this may be all the communication required. Once management obtains the documents and you record that in your workpapers, the issue will be resolved and documented in the audit workpapers.

If a large number of documents are missing, your presentation of the facts to management will also include a discussion of the procedures used to obtain and record required documentation. In this case, you will continue beyond presenting and correcting immediate problems to initiating discussion about how to prevent the situation from recurring.

Throughout these steps, you should be starting to develop outlines that may be used in the audit report. Ongoing communication is best handled by sharing copies of appropriate workpapers with management or by summarizing your conclusions on Comment Worksheets such as those presented in Chapter 2. Summary worksheets are efficient communication tools, fulfilling several purposes. They document your own work for your files, they convey factual information to management briefly, and they allow space for you to record management's action or response. They also serve as the basis for writing the report. By the time fieldwork is complete, you will have a set of outlines from which to select and consolidate material and write the content of the report.

At the close of an audit, you will meet with management to recap the audit results and reach final agreement on action to be taken. For this meeting, you will need either an outline of conclusions and supporting evidence or a draft of the audit report. Preparing an outline or drafting the report before the meeting is critical to ensuring smooth communication during and after the meeting. If you go into the meeting with detailed comment sheets and raw facts and summarize them only after your meetings, you run the risk of changing the tone or focus of an issue you already described to management in different terms. Your preparation for the closing meeting should enable you to convey conclusions to management as you expect them to appear in the report.

Preparation for the meeting involves these steps:

1. Consolidate all Comment Worksheets written during fieldwork, looking for related themes, causes, or effects.

2. Select the significant and unresolved items that you will present in the report. File resolved and less significant items with your workpapers.

3. Write outlines of each comment you will report, using Comment Worksheets and carefully choosing the language, tone, and emphasis appropriate for the report.

4. Write the Conclusion.

Completing these preparatory steps will help you to better accomplish the goal of the meeting: reaching agreement on conclusions, their significance, and action. To prepare management for the meeting, you should prepare an outline of the key comments you will be discussing. If time permits, distribute the outline beforehand as an agenda. If time is short, you can present it at the start of the meeting. The outline should be brief, and should include the following elements for each comment:

- Condition or conclusion

- Evidence (summarized, if possible, in bulleted items or tables or charts)

- Solution or action (if already agreed upon)

For issues on which you have not reached agreement, you can include a recommendation or you can leave that section open, encouraging discussion on appropriate corrective action.

You can use this same outline to run the meeting, working off of it as a handout, overhead, or flip chart. This keeps the discussion clearly on track, working through one item at a time.

As the meeting progresses, be sure to record any changes made during discussion in the language or emphasis of the condition statements or the substance of the supporting evidence. This will enable you to convey the correct tone, emphasis, and language in your report and avoid any rebuttals from management. Your report has to reflect the agreements reached during this meeting. For example, perhaps your draft condition reads, "Management does not approve all purchase orders issued by the department." Your discussions may clarify this issue so that it is restated as: "Supervisors have authority to approve purchase orders under $5,000." Your report must state the revised sentence in the same words and tone to which you agreed during the meeting.

You should also be recording agreements reached on solutions to problems: These will be the action steps included in the written report.

After agreeing on specific comments, you can then recap the meeting with your overall conclusion, addressing the audit objectives. For audits with primarily positive results, you may have chosen to present the conclusion at the start of the meeting, giving recognition to the positive results and then leading into the problem areas.

While some auditors choose to present the draft report to management at this stage, that technique can be problematic. First, a narrative report used as a discussion document causes meeting participants to focus on reading the report rather than talking to each other. Notice where eyes are turned when you work off of a report in a meeting. For 70% of the time, they are focused downward, on the paper. In contrast, when you use an outline along with an overhead or flip chart, eyes are focused upward 70% of the time, leading to more participation. Second, the auditor may rely on the report as a crutch, reading the comments rather than discussing them. Finally, the content or tone of that draft may change as a result of discussion. If you have taken the time to polish the sentences, style, and grammar of a draft, that time may have been wasted if the substance changes. Outlines corresponding to the tone and sequence of the report are usually more productive and efficient documents for the closing meeting.

Written Report to Line Management

Immediately after the closing meeting, you are ready to write the report. Most of the work has already been done, so this step should be completed quickly. With your outline and your notations from the

128

meeting in hand, you can flesh out your ideas into complete narratives, adding the introductory and other administrative sections you need for the final report. For a report of five or fewer pages, this should take about a half-day to a day to compose. Longer reports may require a day or two. Allowing a few days for audit management's review of the draft, the report should be in the hands of line management within a week after the closing meeting.

Management should now have a chance to respond to the report before it is distributed to senior management. Some audit departments request a written response, and then incorporate this into the report before it goes to senior management. The response is either inserted at the back of the audit report, or individual responses are inserted after each comment.

If you have reached substantial agreement in the closing meeting, a written response is not necessary, as you will have already documented actions and disagreements in the draft report. In this case, you should allow management time to react to the accuracy and wording of the final report. A period of about five days is sufficient for management to inquire about anything they perceive as ambiguous or inaccurate.

Report to Senior Management

Once you have line management's agreement with the report, you can distribute copies to senior management. Following the timeliness standards used for reporting to line management, the report should be in senior management's hands two to three weeks after the closing meeting. The distribution list for the report typically includes the next several levels of management above the line manager, the chairman's office, and the external auditors.

The primary purpose of this communication step is to keep division and group executives informed of the performance of the areas under their responsibility. You may also use this reporting phase to gain support for correcting any items that remained unresolved with line management.

Distributing copies of audit reports is the most common way of communicating audit results to senior management, but some organizations use effective alternatives. Depending on the size of your organization and the level of detail executive managers want, you may choose to write monthly or bimonthly summaries for corporate management, including the most senior executives and the chairman's office. Monthly summaries would include the following items for audits under each senior manager's area of responsibility:

- Conclusion, summary, and most significant comments for each audit completed during the period.

- List or summary of significant unresolved items.

- Audits planned for the next period.

In addition to the standard forms of reporting, you may occasionally need to use interim reports or memos. A significant, highly sensitive, or fraudulent issue needs to be brought to management's attention immediately, not three to six weeks after it is identified. When such a situation occurs, it should be reported to senior management right after you have presented and discussed the issue with line management.

Report to the Audit Committee

In its role as overseer, the Audit Committee needs to be kept informed about planned and actual audit coverage, significant audit results, and the resolutions to any identified problems. The purpose of your communication at this level is to assure the Audit Committee that internal controls are appropriate and effective, and that any gaps in the control system are being acted upon. Summary reports are used to keep the Audit Committee informed and to supplement your oral discussions.

While some Audit Committees request a copy of each audit report, most prefer summaries of significant results. Summary reports are written to correspond to the frequency of meetings with the committee, so they are often produced quarterly.

If you have structured your report according to the format suggested in Chapter 8, the bulk of your report to the Audit Committee can be drawn from the introductory pages of each audit report. The quarterly report should include:

- Conclusion for each audit completed.
- Summary of significant unresolved items.

A conclusion written according to the guidelines in Chapter 7 will give the Audit Committee the key information they need: compliance or noncompliance with the major control objectives for each area, significant weaknesses, and management's completed or planned action to resolve problems. Adding a reference to unresolved items keeps the committee aware of existing exposures and may motivate members to intervene on serious issues.

In addition to the results of audit testing, the Audit Committee should be kept aware of your coverage of the corporation. Including a one-page list of audits completed and their relationship to the plan is sufficient to fulfill this objective. Any major change in the audit plan should be explained.

Finally, the internal auditors should issue an annual report to the Audit Committee for the purpose of assessing the overall condition of controls over the last year summarizing the performance of the internal audit staff, and planning the next year's coverage.

An evaluation of controls should be written for each major area of the organization. In a page or less, you can describe your assessment of the control strengths, weaknesses, and exposures for each area, highlighting areas requiring special audit and management attention over the next year.

The performance of the internal audit staff should be summarized to enable the Audit Committee to evaluate the staff qualifications and the sufficiency of audit work. This section should include:

- A brief description of risk analysis or other method used to schedule audit coverage,

- A report on accomplishment of the prior year's audit plan,

- A summary of achievement of internal audit's development and performance objectives, and

- A summary of staff qualifications: experience, education, certification.

Finally, you will report your audit plan for the coming year.

At each upward step in your communication with management, you will be condensing the amount of detail and putting more emphasis on risks and solutions. Line management needs ongoing communication and sufficient detail to take prompt corrective action. Senior management requires immediate knowledge of significant items and periodic summaries of audit conclusions and line management's solutions. The Audit Committee needs assurance that control systems operate as intended and that audit coverage is sufficient to guard against unreasonable exposure. At each reporting step, address your communication to its unique purpose and work off of a reporting structure layered for your multiple audiences. This approach will keep your communications effective, timely, and efficient.

USING
EFFECTIVE STYLE

10

Choosing an Appropriate Style

The choice of writing style is something many auditors do not even consider as they write. "Style?" they might ask if this topic were raised. "I'm just concentrating on getting my ideas across and then getting my boss to sign off on this report without rewriting it. I don't think about style."

When the topic is brought to their attention, auditors may conclude that while style may not be a conscious decision as they write, it certainly does come into play as reports are edited. Their bosses, it seems, have their own personal styles and impose them on report drafts by changing words, adding or deleting phrases, or repositioning information.

Style is most often perceived as a matter of personal preference, the result of favored words, frequently used sentence structures, and comfortable phrasing. A writer's style may be described as formal, direct and simple, academic, verbose, friendly, or terse. Once a writer is classified as having a certain style, readers may come to expect the same manner of expression in all his or her work. There is a certain sound the reader anticipates.

Perceiving style is easier than defining it, however, and even easier still than selecting an appropriate style for your own writing. In business writing, good style may even seem superfluous and not worth the time it takes to polish a report to perfect form. Creative word choice and smooth sentence flow are reserved for literary compositions. Business communications are functional tools, getting a message across to a wide audience.

Communicating a message, though, inevitably involves style. You may become aware of how you alter style according to the type of message you are conveying when you think about forms of writing other than audit reports. When you write a thank-you note or a letter of congratulations, you are likely to use a personal and warm style, preferring simpler words and avoiding formality. If you compose a letter of complaint, you are likely to be blunt, even demanding of action. For a memo to your boss requesting additional resources—staff, time, budget—you may use more diplomatic word choice and suggest alternatives rather than demand one solution. These differences all reflect style choices. They may seem unconscious, or they may occur naturally when you compose for a particular audience, but they are deliberate choices designed to convey your message in the most appropriate style. It would certainly be inappropriate, and ineffective, to use a blunt and demanding style in a memo to your boss. You would be more likely to offend than to win cooperation. On the other hand, a soft, diplomatic letter of complaint may not get a response.

Depending on the significance of the message you are conveying to management and the tone you want to express, the style of audit writing may also vary from one report to another. By becoming aware of stylistic differences and the particular writing techniques contributing to style, you can be a more versatile writer, adjusting your expressions to best get your message across to the right audience.

As a first step in achieving flexibility, you must recognize that business writing is a product of habit. Then you must discipline yourself to break the bad habits you may have acquired.

Proof of the habitual nature of writing audit reports comes from their predictability. Without any knowledge of an internal audit department, I can pick up a stack of its reports and accurately predict certain language. I can tell you that I am likely to read about "control weaknesses," "items that deserve management's attention," and "recommendations to enhance control." I am likely to hear that "the auditors found" certain "exceptions," that "deficiencies were noted," and that "the review disclosed opportunities for improvement." I can also guess that some of the "findings" will be about "lack of segregation of duties," "untimely reconciliation of accounts," and "lack of formal operating procedures." It is a safe bet the auditors will recommend that "management develop and implement procedures" and point out that the identified weaknesses must be corrected because they "increase exposure."

The result of such predictability is boredom. Consider your senior managers or Audit Committee members who read every audit report. Are they seeing the same words in every report? If so, they are seeing little originality. Instead, they are rereading phrases that have dominated the audit vocabulary for decades. These phrases may be comfortable to writers for the same reasons they are boring to readers—they are safe, noncontroversial, and proven. They are easy to write, because they require little more than a quick revision of earlier reports. They are diplomatic, because they provide a cushion before the findings, or negative conclusions, are offered.

To avoid sounding predictable, to step out of the safe haven of audit vocabulary, you must resolve to weed out the jargon from your writing and to plant more original words and more creative presentations. Once you stop relying on set phrases, your own style will emerge naturally. It is sometimes frightening to give up the comfortable language, wondering what you will use instead, but you will be rewarded with a greater opportunity for originality, a more inviting rhythm and flow to your writing, and a more fitting match between your word choice and the tone of the message you want to convey.

Although exact techniques will vary from one person to another, the following guidelines can help you achieve a more effective and inviting style:

- Make a deliberate choice of style.
- Use active verbs.
- Use your own words.
- Vary the sound of your language.

Make a Deliberate Choice of Style

The three comments that follow are each written in a different style. Identify the comment that comes closest to your own way of writing.

Comment 1
"Based on the limited sample, it was noted that controls may not be adequate to ensure that reconciliations are performed in a timely manner and that account balances are accurate."

137

Comment 2

"It appears that procedures are not in place to assure that accounts are reconciled in a timely manner and that account balances are maintained accurately."

Comment 3

"Accounting does not reconcile the accounts daily, allowing the potential for inaccuracies in financial reports."

About 75% of auditors asked to respond to similar style choices select comments 1 and 2 as most representative of their own writing. On the other hand, when the same auditors are asked to select the comment they like best, about 90% select comment 3. "It is direct, clear, to the point, easy to read," they say. Then why do auditors more often write in the styles of comments 1 and 2? Habit. Safety. Comfort. These are reasons writers give for their choice of styles. When asked to describe comments 1 and 2, writers are likely to choose terms such as "wordy," "indirect," "passive". Some go further, describing comment 1 as "wimpy," "indecisive," or "uncertain." Comment 3, they say, conveys a different tone. It shows a writer who is confident and a report that is conclusive.

It is the style of each of the three comments that influences the reader's image of the writer. Comments 1 and 2 show a passive, indirect style resulting from these writing techniques:

- Passive voice,
- Qualifiers,
- Impersonal words, and
- Wordiness.

Comment 3 reflects a forceful, direct writing style, using these techniques:

- Active voice,
- No qualifiers or cushioning phrases, and
- Conciseness.

The irony of business writing is that readers want the direct, forceful style, but writers are reluctant to use it. To reach a greater balance between the interests of readers and the style of writers, we

138

will concentrate in this chapter on techniques for achieving the direct style. This will allow you to choose your style more deliberately, reserving the passive technique for the limited number of situations where it will be more effective.

Making a choice of style requires you to think about your audience, the likely reaction to your message, and your degree of confidence in your conclusion. John S. Fielden, a professor and consultant on management communication, gives this advice: "To get your message across, vary your writing style to suit each situation you have to deal with."*

The passive, indirect style is appropriate only when:

- Limitations of audit testing do not allow you to express a direct conclusion.

- Tact and diplomacy are required to gain cooperation from management.

- Sensitivities are strong and a direct style is perceived as too blunt.

The times these criteria are met will be few. That means that most of your writing will be more appropriately presented in the direct style. This may cause a turnaround from your usual pattern. As your guiding rule, write first in the direct style. Then, if the situation warrants, revise to the passive.

The rest of this chapter suggests additional techniques for a forceful, direct style.

Use Active Verbs

The active voice is fundamental to conciseness, clarity, and directness. To achieve a direct writing style, you must build sentences on the foundation of active verbs and build reports around active sentences. Active sentences are those in which a subject acts. Put simply, these sentences follow the sequence of subject-verb-object. For example, in comment 3 above, the sentence is active: "Accounting does not reconcile the accounts daily." The sentence has an active subject—

---

*John S. Fielden, "What Do You Mean You Don't Like My Style?" *Harvard Business Review*, May-June 1982, pp. 128-138.

"accounting"—performing an action—"does not reconcile"— on a particular object—"the accounts."

In contrast, the passive voice presents a subject being acted upon. "Reconciliations are not performed in a timely manner" is a passive sentence. The subject—"reconciliations"—is passive. It is not doing anything, but rather it is being acted upon. You can recognize the active voice by looking for a principle verb form expressing action and usually written in one word. For instance, "The branch *receives* deposits," "Managers *approve* the form," "The department does not *confirm* balances," "We *recommend.*" Passive verbs always require a form of the verb "to be" along with a past participle. "Deposits are *received* by the branch," "The forms *are approved* by management," "Balances *are not confirmed,*" "*It is recommended.*"

The active voice, by requiring a subject and verb, is automatically more precise. The passive voice does not require identification of the subject -the person or party performing the action - and in many cases that information is left out, as in "Balances are not confirmed." This passive sentence does not answer the question, "By whom?" It is imprecise and unclear. Even when a prepositional phrase is added to identify the subject, as in "Deposits are received by the branch," the passive voice is still more wordy than the active. Active verbs and sentences—"The branch receives the deposits," "The Accounting Department does not reconcile the accounts"—are the key to a direct, clear, and inviting writing style.

The next two contrasting paragraphs convey the stylistic differences between the passive and active voices. The first paragraph, which is passive, is monotonous and drawn out. The second, active, paragraph is more concise and has a smoother flow of information.

Passive

The trading operations area was not centralized. Processing of trading activities was handled by various departments. Foreign Exchange and Precious Metals trading transactions were processed by the Foreign Operations Department. Banknotes, Money Desk and Bond transactions were processed by the Domestic Operations Department.

Active

The bank had decentralized trading operations. Foreign Operations handled Foreign Exchange and Precious Metals, with Banknotes, Money Desk, Bond transactions being processed by Domestic Operations.

Chapter 11, "Writing Concisely," gives more pointers on reducing the use of passive verbs in your reports.

Writing in the active voice raises a direct conflict with another tradition of internal audit reporting—the impersonal style. To keep reports constructive, auditors have been told, they must keep their writing impersonal. The guiding principle is to avoid personal references to negative issues. It is certainly true that you will get a better response from the statement "Accounts were not reconciled" than from the declaration "John Smith did not reconcile the accounts." The assignment of personal responsibility is seen as accusatory. Unfortunately, this rule of impersonality gets carried to an extreme. Some audit managers even forbid personal pronouns—for example "you" and "we"—in their effort to remain impersonal. The preference for the active voice will force you to identify subjects and use personal pronouns. "It is recommended" must become "We recommend" in the active voice. "An audit was completed," has to be written as "We audited."

While remembering not to name names responsible for audit findings, free yourself from the rule of impersonal style. Use personal pronouns when referring to your own work or addressing your reader directly. (For example, "We will appreciate your response to this report by April 2.") Avoid awkward third-person references such as "The auditors completed a review," "Internal auditing recommends," or "Management response indicated that......."

The impersonal approach conveys a tone of detachment. It sounds as if audit results and recommendations are developed from a distance. Here is an illustration:

Passive, Impersonal Style

It was noted that the disposition of redeemed certificates of deposit was not adequately documented on a consistent basis. It is recommended that the Bank document the disposition of redeemed certificates of deposit on the face of the cancelled certificate to provide an adequate audit trail of the disposition of the funds.

Active, Personal Style

The branch did not consistently document the disposition of redeemed certificates of deposit. We recommend that the bank record this information on the face of the certificate to allow for tracing of funds.

As evidence of the habitual nature of the impersonal technique, look at this excerpt from a memo an auditor wrote to her staff:

Field testing regarding vault securities will begin July 1. All assigned personnel should report to the staff room at 8:00 a.m. that morning. Vault management will hold a meeting at that time. The following policies and procedures should be adhered to by audit personnel.

The memo would be much easier to understand if written more personally:

Please report to the staff room at 8:00 a.m. on July 1 for a meeting on field testing of vault securities. During this fieldwork, please adhere to the following procedures.

Build your writing on an active, personal sentence structure. Define subjects, choose action verbs, and use personal pronouns.

Use Your Own Words

Relying on traditional audit language to compose a report results in an unnatural, uncreative, and uninformative style. Certain ubiquitous phrases appear from one audit department to the next, such as "During the audit, the following control weaknesses were noted." How can so many writers in so many different places select the exact same words to express their conclusion? Is this the spontaneous generation of creative thought? Hardly. Traditional, overused phrases are not creative. Because they are overused, they have turned into generalizations that have lost any precise meaning. They are uninformative and they are not the natural expressions of an individual. The same auditors who wrote the sentence in the example above surely would not have used this same expression if senior management took them aside, spoke to them in confidence, and asked them their candid evaluation of one of the company's operations.

Your words should be natural, original, and precise. Although report writing cannot be as informal and choppy as conversation, the words you choose should sound like something you would say. To convey your own style, do not rely on cliches, jargon, or pretentious language. State your exact message, using words that are meaningful and descriptive to you and your reader.

Avoid Overused Phrases. With overuse, a word or phrase becomes a cliche, familiar but void of meaning. Trite expressions may have had a clear meaning when first used, but have lost their precision by being applied to a wide variety of situations. The following phrases have become cliches in audit report writing.

Audit Cliches

"Management should ensure that proper procedures and controls are in effect."

"For control purposes, proper documentation should be maintained."

"It is the bank's policy that all branches develop documented EDP standards for the effective and efficient utilization of EDP resources."

"Lack of segregation of duties compromises internal control."

"The integrity of the system is not assured."

"Management should develop formal written procedures and then ensure that procedures are implemented and complied with."

"This practice represents an exposure to the bank."

"Assets should be adequately safeguarded."

"Implementation of the recommendations will enhance control."

"Several deficiencies were noted in the operation."

Avoid such cliches and use more descriptive substitutes. Rather than saying "enhance control," give examples of the exact benefits management will achieve. Instead of "an exposure," define the risk.

As a replacement for "develop and document procedures," state the specific procedure you expect management to follow.

In the following examples, notice how the ambiguity of the sentences with cliches is changed to a precise message by substituting more exact words.

Cliche: Informal communication exists between the system administrator and department heads.

Precise: Department heads do not notify the system administrator in writing of employee transfers.

Cliche: Records are not adequately safeguarded.

Precise: Records are left unattended outside the office.

Cliche: There is no audit trail of users with XXX authority.

Precise: Activities of users with unlimited access to the data base are not tracked.

Cliche: A review of the payroll system revealed internal control problems related to wages paid to several operating departments.

Precise: Employee salaries are not within established salary levels.

Do Not Use Overstated Language. Fancy, complex, or overblown words do not embellish your idea; they mask it. What is the key idea in each of the following sentences?

"Prior audits of this subject identified unsatisfactory revenue effecting conditions."

"The responsibility is to manage subsidiary organization to effect desired current return on equity while causing inherent corporate value to appreciate by virtue of the value of its future income potential."

"Pursuant to our telephonic communication, I have advised you that the accountant has advised the undersigned that Form XLMX is not necessary in the above referenced matter."

"The ability to use data base technology effectively relies on well-defined and enforced standards and procedures that are consistently applied."

In each case, the simple idea underlying each sentence is hidden by extraneous and overstated language. The result of these expressions is a confused, alienated, or lost reader.

Express your ideas naturally, in a way that communicates easily to your reader. Avoid stiff language and contrived phrases you would not use in conversation. Here are examples of overstated paragraphs and their simpler revisions.

Overstated: It is the nature of traditional data base administration to require a central data base management function to ensure that controls and procedures for all data bases are implemented in a consistent manner. In this way the technical and business advantages of this complicated and highly structured data file method can be developed and coordinated among multiple application systems.

Revision: Central data base management is necessary to control the consistency of data among applications, properly restrict access, and efficiently manage data storage.

Overstated: We recommend that management determine and establish a dollar limit on funding checks, whereby any checks above this limit would require dual signatures. We further suggest that one of these two signatures be from a management level above the current signer's and that accounting personnel's check-signing authorization be revoked.

Revision: Management should require dual signatures for checks above a set limit, with one of the signers at the department-manager level. Personnel should not be authorized to sign checks.

> *Overstated:* We recommend immediate implementation of a system enhancement that establishes the five-digit authorization number as a bonafide, functional control. Implementation of this control alone would greatly reduce the potential exposure.
>
> *Revision:* A five-digit authorization number should be required to process entries. This will reduce the possibility of unauthorized persons entering transactions.

Vague words and general language combine with cliches and overstatements to diminish the clarity of reports. Rather than generalizing, state specific facts, give examples, or describe any ambiguous terms. Choose concrete, tangible words over the abstract or vague. Here is an example of an auditor's generalization.

> We noted during testing and through discussions with the sales finance staff that copies of signed financial documents are not being forwarded to merchants on a timely basis.

"Timely basis" can be made more specific by stating facts. How long does it take to forward the documents? What standard of timeliness should be applied? Such facts are essential if management is to reach agreement on this comment and take acceptable action. The auditor, continuing with ambiguous language, recommended that the financial documents be forwarded "within a reasonable period of time." It will be hard for that auditor and for bank management to determine if the response to this recommendation is acceptable. "Reasonable time" can be defined differently by many different readers.

Vague language in a recommendation is especially weak, as it leaves so much room for interpretation. Consider another example: "The aged suspense account analysis should be prepared on a consistent basis, with stronger emphasis on follow-up."

What constitutes consistency? And how would we measure a "stronger emphasis" on follow-up? Give examples of action that should be taken. "The analysis should be done monthly" is direct, specific, and measurable. "Requests for explanations of items should be tracked and followed up on weekly" gives an example of what might be meant by "stronger emphasis." When you choose language, think of creating a picture in the reader's mind. Give your audience words they can envision, or describe actions they can measure. Here are examples.

> *Vague:* The response Accounting receives is sometimes inadequate.
>
> *Specific:* Responses do not always list the planned action and estimated completion date.
>
> *Vague:* Confusion exists at the branches as to where the form should be sent.
>
> *Specific:* Half the branches send the form to Branch Administration, while the others send it to their divisional headquarters.
>
> *Vague:* In several instances employee salaries were above/below the established range.
>
> *Specific:* Twenty percent of salaries tested were above the established range, and eight percent were below.
>
> *Vague:* The files contained insufficient documentation of approvals.
>
> *Specific:* The files did not show the department manager's approval.

Limit the Use of Technical and Esoteric Language. Remember that you are writing to a broad and diverse audience. Your readers among senior management and the Audit Committee have varying backgrounds and different levels of understanding of the technical terms used throughout your organization. You must bridge these differences by using language understandable to your readers and, where necessary, by defining unknown terms.

Writers show awareness of this need to inform their readers by diligently spelling out acronyms the first time they use them. This step, while necessary, is of only limited value in keeping reports free of technical jargon. To keep your style inviting while presenting complex issues, you must define acronyms and technical names in terms of their function, prefer simple over esoteric descriptions, and refrain from becoming too simplistic or explanatory.

The next paragraph shows how a writer carefully spells out an acronym, but still leaves the reader unclear of the exact subject.

> QMF, Query Management Facility, lacks backout and recovery capabilities and proper editing features that standard application language provide.

Although QMF is spelled out, a lay reader does not know the function of Query Management Facility. What does it do? Here is a revision that better defines the term for the reader.

> Query Management Facility (QMF), used to create ad hoc reports, does not have the backout, recovery, and editing features provided by standard application programs.

By defining what Query Management Facility does, the revised sentence becomes more informative and easier for the reader to understand.

In addition to defining unknown terms, you must also know when to use simpler language in place of them. Sometimes, a more straightforward explanation is better than a detailed technical one. For an illustration of this idea, consider the following paragraph.

> There are weak system controls over IMS. Currently, terminals are system generated for certain trancodes. This process establishes a restriction on the functions that can be performed at a terminal to those prescribed by the specified trancodes. Personnel who have been newly reassigned to the Branch now have terminals that are "gen'd" for a trancode that allows for all functions (account opening, closing, and maintenance functions).

The technical language obscures the message of the paragraph. A more straightforward revision makes the idea clear.

> Branch personnel are able to open, close, and make changes to account data because their teller terminals do not restrict access to any of these functions.

148

In the effort to define terms for their readers, writers run the risk of becoming too simplistic or explanatory, spelling out detail the reader does not need. Here is an explanation that causes rather than eliminates confusion.

> The remote job entry site is basically a remote data entry and printing site with limited remote job entry and distributed processing functions. It is part of the company's on-line electronic data processing network and represents a window into the centralized data processing mainframe computer systems. As an access point within the overall network, it is important for the RJE Center to have adequate controls in order to protect the entire network.

The **above** explanation does not tell the readers anything they do not already know. By using overstated language in this background information, the writer complicates the issue. The term "remote job entry" is self-explanatory and can stand on its own.

Vary the Sound of Your Language

Repetition is tiring. The same words, the same sentence structure throughout a report lead to a monotonous rhythm, making it difficult for readers to maintain interest. When readers start losing interest, they start skimming your report instead of reading it attentively. Thinking that they are about to reread the same information, they may skip a paragraph. Seeing phrases repeated, they may choose to browse through a page. Such lack of attention may cause readers to miss important information.

Your first step to achieving variety is to look for and eliminate repetition of words or phrases throughout a page or section of your report. As you read the examples that follow, circle the words used repeatedly.

> **Example 1:**
> It was noted that formal reconciliations between the computer balance and the general ledger control account for interest payable on NOW and Money Market accounts were not performed. The Bank should prepare formal reconcili-

ations between the computer balance and the general ledger control account for interest payable on NOW and Money Market accounts and investigate any discrepancies.

Dormant demand deposit and savings accounts signature cards were filed with signature cards on active accounts. As dormant accounts are susceptible to internal fraud, the Bank should physically segregate dormant account signature cards.

Example 2:

Because the collection process is not rotated periodically between Bank personnel, a Bank officer should periodically review collections. The supervisor should particularly take note of any late payments and determine that tracers or inquiries were issued for the items. This review should be documented.

Once you have identified repeated words, eliminate them by combining sentences, selecting synonyms, or using pronouns. For instance, here is a revision of Example 1.

The Bank does not reconcile interest payable on NOW and Money Market accounts between the computer balance and the general ledger. These two balances should be reconciled, with any discrepancies investigated.

Signature cards for dormant accounts are filed along with those for active accounts. Since inactive accounts are susceptible to internal fraud, the Bank should segregate these signature cards.

When synonyms and pronouns are used, they must be placed as close as possible to the nouns they describe to maintain clarity of meaning. In the first paragraph above, "these two balances" follows immediately after "the computer balance and the general ledger," making it clear what the pronoun "these" refers to. In the second paragraph, "inactive accounts" is used as a synonym for the phrase "dormant accounts" in the previous sentence.

The repetition in Example 2 can be eliminated by combining sentences.

Because collections are not rotated, a Bank officer should periodically review this process, taking note of late payments, determining that tracers or inquiries were issued. The officer should document this review.

The same sentence structure becomes monotonous, too. In the next excerpt, every sentence contains a passive verb structure. Even though the writer has included some introductory phrases to break the monotony, the result is still choppy and repetitive. The revision combines sentences and changes structures to create a more inviting flow.

Example:

During our review of Daily Activity Reports produced throughout the audit period we noted these are reconciled to trading desk positions by the trading operations. Identified differences are verbally discussed and corrected with trading desk traders. The daily position reconciliations were not documented or filed during most of the audit period. Commencing February the position reconciliations were appropriately documented and filed. We commend your efforts to improve controls over daily position reconciliations and recommend these always be documented and maintained.

Revision:

During the audit period, trading operations was reconciling Daily Activity Reports to trading desk positions without documenting the reconciliation and resolution of differences. They began keeping this documentation in February, and we recommend that this practice be continued.

Repositioning information in a sentence can also change the emphasis. Consider how the next three sentences provide slightly different interpretations of the information.

Version 1:

As previously reported, there is continued pressure on profits across all domestic units as reported losses are $50 million year-to-date with XYZ being the only unit reporting profits.

151

Version 2:

Reported losses are $50 million year-to-date, with XYZ being the only unit reporting profit. This puts continued pressure on all units for greater profit.

Version 3:

Pressure exists for all domestic units to produce profits. Reported losses are $50 million year-to-date, and XYZ is the only unit reporting profit.

In version 1, the writer sandwiches the key piece of information—losses of $50 million—into the middle of the sentence, detracting attention from it. A clever construction if the goal is to bury bad news in the hope the reader will not find it. In most cases, the writer's goal is to emphasize the key idea. To do that, the emphatic statement should appear at the beginning or end of the sentence, not in the middle. In version 2, the repositioning of the loss to the beginning calls attention to that main idea. Similarly, in version 3, the same idea of loss appears at the start of the second sentence.

Eliminating repetition, combining sentences, changing structures, and considering emphasis will create greater variety in your writing. These techniques will make your narrative flow more smoothly, carrying readers along through your thought pattern and not allowing them to get sidetracked or, worse yet, lost. Originality of word choice results from breaking out of bad habits, avoiding worn-out language, and using your own best judgment in presenting ideas.

By becoming aware of the stylistic habits in your own writing, you can gain control of the sound and tone of your reports. Most important, you can choose the style you want to use. Instead of relying on the traditional passive, indirect style of writing, you can select a more forceful and direct style, using the techniques that go along with it. You can get your message across clearly and simply. In those delicate or uncertain situations, you can still use more passive or indirect writing techniques.

11

Writing
Concisely

"There are always too many words at first," asserts Jacques Barzun,[*] a conclusion all good writers come to when reviewing their work. As writers struggle to clarify, narrow, and better define their thoughts, they include many of their empty, ambiguous, and redundant musings in their first drafts. Crisp, concise phrases expressing the writer's exact meaning are always harder to write than the verbose, rambling explanation. So writers start off on the easy path, using comfortable but unnecessary phrases, relying on cliches and overused expressions, and expanding simple ideas into complicated phrases.

To omit needless words from your reports, you must be able to recognize symptoms and causes of wordiness, evaluate your own writing styles and habits, and edit your work carefully. You must learn to choose the brief phrase over the longer one, the simpler term over the more complex, and the direct statement over the indirect. Most importantly, you must value the clarity of a brief, precise sentence over the number of pages in your report.

This writing sample will help you begin to recognize signs of wordiness:

```
This report describes the functions of Worldwide Investment
Management, Inc. (WIMI), which is a wholly owned registered
investment advisory subsidiary of Worldwide Corporation.
WIMI performs the investment management function for
institutional investment accounts of Worldwide through
```

*Jacques Barzun, *Simple & Direct: A Rhetoric for Writers,* Revised Edition (New York: Harper & Row, 1985), p. 196.

a service agreement with the Corporation. It should be noted that the management of fiduciary accounts and the proper exercise of Worldwide's fiduciary powers is monitored by the Global Investment Committee (GIC). GIC is a committee responsible for approving the opening and closing of accounts and conducting initial reviews of new accounts. The committee also conducts annual reviews of the investments held in each account for continued merit. The use of finan-cial futures and options and other new products is also reviewed by this committee.

Here are the editor's comments on this narrative:

~~This report describes the functions of~~ Worldwide Investment Management, Inc. (WIMI), ~~which is a~~ (n) ~~wholly owned registered~~ investment advisory subsidiary of Worldwide Corporation. ~~WIMI performs the investment~~ management ~~function for~~ institutional investment accounts ~~of Worldwide through a service agreement with the Corporation. It should be noted that the management of fiduciary accounts and the proper exercise of~~ (Worldwide's fiduciary powers) ~~is monitored by~~ the Global Investment Committee (GIC). ~~GIC is a committee~~ responsible for approving ~~the~~ opening and closing ~~of accounts and conducting initial~~ reviews of new accounts. ~~The committee also conducts annual~~ reviews ~~of the~~ investments held in each account; ~~for continued merit. The use of~~ financial futures and options and other new products ~~is also reviewed by this committee.~~

The editorial comments show the causes of wordiness in this paragraph:

Filler phrases:	This report describes . . . It should be noted that . . .
Expanded modifiers:	. . . which is a wholly owned . . .
Drawn-out verbs:	. . . performs the investment management function . . .

154

Passive voice:	The management . . . is monitored by the GIC.
Repetition:	. . . the Global Investment Committee (GIC). GIC is a committee....
Extra articles and prepositions:	. . . the opening and closing of accounts.

By recognizing and avoiding these common causes of wordiness in your reports, you can write more directly, concisely, and clearly, holding your readers' attention with every word.

Causes of Wordiness

Filler Phrases

To get started, writers often warm up by beginning their sentences with comfortable, predictable phrases that lead into the main thought. These cushioning phrases, putting a space between the reader and the message, add unneeded words and slow down communication of the key point. They provide no content and simply take up space on the paper. These lead-ins may be functional when composing the first draft. It is easy to write, "This report describes the functions of . . . ." The writer hardly needs to think about his or her ideas before getting words down on paper and, almost instantaneously, the first draft is begun. For readers, though, filler phrases clutter the report, stating the obvious, needlessly referring to the writer, or labeling a preceding or following thought.

Stating the Obvious. Writers sometimes waste words by describing context that is obvious from the title of the report. In the earlier example, it was not necessary to begin by saying, "This report describes the functions of Worldwide Investment Management, Inc.," when the report is titled "Worldwide Investment Management, Inc."

Wherever possible, let the report title or section heading speak for you, and be careful not to repeat such information in another sentence. Common examples of restating the title or subject line include:

> The purpose of this letter is to provide you with information on our new account services.
>
> *Revision:* Subject: New Account Services
>
> ---
>
> Our objectives in auditing Accounts Payable were to. . .
>
> *Revision:* Objectives: . . . .

Even more cumbersome are phrases that directly state what is easily understood from the title and format of the report itself. Look at these examples from a report titled " Auditing Report: Accounts Payable":

> We have recently completed an audit of Accounts Payable.
>
> The audit testing revealed the following internal control weaknesses.
>
> Some exceptions were disclosed in Accounts Payable.
>
> Accounts Payable procedures need improvement.
>
> During our review of Accounts Payable, it was noted that . . .

The title "Audit Report: Accounts Payable" says everything these phrases restate. It is obvious to the readers that the audit was "recently completed," that "audit tests disclosed" the results presented in the report, that "exceptions were noted" and "procedures need improvement," and that the findings were "revealed."

The following paragraph illustrates how a writer adds many extra words by describing what is already understood.

> We suggest that cash collateral procedures relative to legal source documents and the monitoring processes be developed/adhered to in order to enhance internal controls and accountability. Our audit encompassed a review of all cash collateral account balances; monitoring and proof procedures; and related documentation requirements. As a result of our analyses, we noted that five accounts were not found on

156

the Cash Collateral Control List when documentation supported such action. On the contrary, documentation for two other accounts could not be found to substantiate their being on said list.

Revision: We suggest establishing procedures for documenting and monitoring cash collateral. Five accounts were missing from the Cash Collateral Control List, and two others on the list did not have required documentation."

Referring to the writer. Put your results, not yourself and your work, in the foreground. Readers are interested in conclusions, and you can emphasize these by removing references to what you did in your testing, what you are doing in the report, or what you think about the information you are presenting. Here is an illustration of a sentence needlessly referring to the writer:

Based on various discussions with representatives of the departments,we believe that the current process should be enhanced, and specify the following: . . .

Almost three lines are taken up with references to what the writer did, what he thinks, and what he is going to say next. Three lines into the paragraph, the reader still does not know the message.
Other examples of unnecessary references include:

As a result, Internal Audit was not able to determine whether or not all cash sales amounts were being transferred in a timely manner.

Revision: There is no assurance that cash sales amounts are transferred promptly.

Subsequent investigation indicated that deduction authorizations had not been initiated.

Revision: Deduction authorizations had not been initiated.

The review also disclosed open purchase orders. **These** purchase orders *were discussed* with management for their subsequent disposition.

Revision: Management resolved open purchase orders during the audit.

We selected a sample of 46 items for testing. Of these items, we *found* that 13 did not include required signatures.

Revision: Thirteen of 46 items tested did not have required signatures.

It is our opinion that these changes should be made.

Revision: These changes should be made.

We recommended and management agreed that the accounts will be verified.

Revision: The accounts will be verified.

We would like to acknowledge the cooperation of the staff.

Revision: Thank you for your cooperation.

Labeling. Avoid putting labels on words that can stand alone. The italic words in the following sentences are unneeded labels.

The fact that the accounts are not reconciled contributes to the errors.

A basic characteristic of cooperative agreements is that they are reciprocal *in nature.*

Verification is an important *type of* control *procedure.*

> Confirmations are done in *the month of* June.

> A *series of* tests was done to evaluate the different *kinds of* accounts.

> *The process of* balancing is one of the clerk's responsibilities.

Statements of the obvious, needless references to the writer, and redundant labels add words to your reports and diminish the strength of the message. They take up valuable space and put a barrier between you and your reader.

Expanded Modifiers

The best descriptions are short, crisp, and clear. Two or three words conveying a precise meaning are more informative than a longer phrase or extra sentence explaining those few words. In business writing, a direct statement is preferable to a drawn-out explanation. To tighten your sentences, examine the value of every word. Can a phrase be reduced to one word? Is there redundancy? Are modifiers unnecessary? Extra modifiers in your writing can create wordiness and bury your stronger nouns and verbs.

Expanded modifiers may appear in reports as adjectives turned to phrases or clauses, redundancies, superfluous words, overstated phrases, or qualifiers.

Adjectives turned to phrases or clauses. When you need a modifier to describe or clarify a noun, choose the one-word adjective that gives the clearest description. Avoid turning that adjective into a phrase or clause, as the writer has done in this sentence:

> The storage facility *that is located at* Central City *and is used by* the software engineering department for storing its magnetic media is inadequate.

The sentence can be made more succinct by eliminating the extra phrases and presenting them as adjectives:

> The Central City storage facility used for magnetic media is inadequate.

Or: Software engineering's storage facility in Central City is inadequate.

Unneeded adjective phrases or clauses often begin with the word "that" or "which." By removing these phrases, sentences become leaner, as illustrated below.

The report that summarizes the quarterly results

Revision: The quarterly summary report

An invoice that is properly approved and verified

Revision: An approved and verified invoice

The log that lists outstanding invoices

Revision: The outstanding-invoice log

Here are other examples of phrases used in place of adjectives:

Procedures related to the investment management function have not been documented.

Revision: Investment-management procedures are not documented.

It is our recommendation that the application form incorporate an area on the application that would require the officer to list the insurer and the appropriate policy number.

Revision: "The form should include an area for the name of the insurer and the policy number.

> The current Post-Audit Status Report maintained by Corporate Purchasing lists all projects for which post-completion audits have been requested and previously not received.
>
> *Revision:* Corporate Purchasing's Post-Audit Status Report lists open requests.

Redundancies. "Say it and say it again" seems to be the philosophy of some writers. They are not satisfied with a one-word description and prefer to include a second modifier expressing the same meaning as the first. For example, an auditor recommended that a department provide managers with "up-to-date information on a timely basis," rather than simply "timely information." Perhaps the writer was distinguishing this from "outdated information on a timely basis." Other auditors write that they performed a "review and analysis," suggesting that some of their reviews may not include analysis. One especially cumbersome construction is: "Our audit included a review and analysis . . . ." In each of these examples, one word will suffice: "review," "analysis," or "audit." Reports often include recommendations to provide "written documentation of procedures." What other type of documentation is there? Some auditors clarify even further, saying that "formalized detailed written documentation should be provided," or "Current procedures have not been formally documented in writing."

Redundant Modifiers

adequately safeguarded

secured by a lock

a single individual

each and every

necessary requirement

still remain

preliminary report containing interim findings

unnecessary risk of loss

written references

processed automatically by computer

161

Superfluous Words. **Rather than letting a word stand on its own, writers sometimes qualify it by attaching an unneeded modifier. For example:**

> The current system for requesting, completing, and verifying follow-up work is not being followed according to Company guidelines.

It would be enough to say:

> Company guidelines for requesting, completing, and verifying follow-up are not followed.

Modifiers that are frequently unnecessary include:

actual	always	currently	specific
all	any	really	
very	certainly	some	

In the following examples, the writers have used superfluous words.

> We selected *a total of* 70 applications for *detailed* testing.
>
> *Audit* procedures *performed* included, *among others,* comparing *actual* processing time to *established* standards.
>
> *Current* forms do not include *the appropriate* account numbers.
>
> To *adequately* monitor this information, . . .
>
> A *formalized* procedure should be developed for backing up all software, including *both* software under development and mature software *that is being maintained.*

Overstated phrases. Choose the simple word over the complicated. Avoid a string of four or five words when one can convey the same meaning.

Examples

Documentation *regarding* policies and procedures *involving the* freight management *function* is not available.

Revision: Documentation of freight management policies and procedures is not available.

Requests are not *being* made *on a timely basis.*

Revision: Requests are not timely.

The lending *function, as it relates to* international customers is performed by the Specialized Lending *group.*

Revision: Specialized Lending handles international loans.

Improper *inclusion or exclusion* of capital expenditures will *overstate or understate* the Company's capital assets.

Revision: Improper reporting of capital expenditures will misstate the Company's capital assets.

Overstated	Direct
at this point in time	now
by means of	by
due to the fact that	because; as a result
for the purpose of	For; to
in an effort to	to
in order to	to
in the event of	if; when
near future	soon
on a monthly basis	monthly
whether or not	whether; if

Qualifiers. The weakest modifiers qualify or limit the writer's message, as the italicized phrases do in the following sentences.

> *Based on the results of the audit tests and procedures performed, it is our opinion, subject to the resolution of the findings and concerns noted above,* that the unit is processing business on an accurate, consistent, and timely basis and that controls over operations are adequate.

> *In some areas,* procedures were not *completely* documented.

> *Existing* controls are not *consistently* followed.

> *In our opinion,* the department is properly following the written strategies developed by management. The monthly evaluation and reassessment of strategies *appears to be* an effective way of keeping up-to-date with the current market conditions. Our review found no exceptions *that require management review.*

> *Given the current situation,* ABC *may be* losing potential customers if this rate is significantly higher than current market rates. Alternatively, we *may be* losing potential revenue if market rates are higher than the established rate or we *may not be* charging sufficient amounts to cover our actual costs.

Drawn-out Verbs

Verbs strengthen your sentences. They describe action: what happened, what the writer or another party has done or is doing, what action management has taken or will take in the future.

One-word action verbs build concise sentences. When you write, try to identify the action of your sentence in one word. Avoid drawing out the verb into a phrase of three or four words. The writer of the following sentence uses five words to express the action: We recommend that management *place increased follow-up attention on* outstanding invoices.

The message is clouded by the string of verbs. "Place" and "increase" are weak verbs, leading into the precise action of "follow-up." The revised sentence, with a concise action verb would read: Management should *follow up* on outstanding invoices.

Writers frequently use drawn-out verbs to increase the length of their sentences and muffle the action word. The following examples show how you can write more clearly and succinctly by using concise verbs.

A determination should be made of the file's materiality in order that *an accrual can be made* of the liability.

Revision: Management should *determine* the file's materiality and *accrue* the liability.

Every effort should be made to streamline procedures in order to comply with regulations requiring payment within 15 days.

Revision: Comply with the policy requiring payment within 15 days.

It was noted that *formal reconciliations* between cash balances and their related imprest balances *are not being prepared.*

Revision: Cash balances and related imprest balances *are not reconciled.*

Testing of back-up media *should be performed on a scheduled basis.*

Revision: Back-up media *should be tested* regularly.

The original sentences show the tendency to express the action in several words: "perform reconciliations," "perform testing," "make a determination." Eliminating these drawn-out verbs from your writing will decrease the length of your sentences and increase the clarity of your thought.

Drawn-out verbs	Concise verbs
arrive at an agreement	agree
conduct an evaluation of	evaluate

Drawn-out verbs	Concise verbs
give consideration to	consider
implement a modification of	modify
make an analysis of	analyze
place emphasis on	emphasize
place restrictions on	restrict
perform a verification of	verify
undertake a review	review

Especially when presenting recommendations, writers seem to back into the action verb. For example:

We recommend that management *establish procedures to ensure that account balances are verified* on a monthly basis.

A shorter and more understandable sentence highlights the requested action:

We recommend that management *verify* account balances monthly.

Or the writer can state the action directly:

Verify account balances monthly.

Here is another example of burying the action word:

Management should implement procedures whereby invoices are compared to the purchase order amounts and ensure that these procedures are being complied with.

A better statement is:

Compare invoices to purchase order amounts.

Finally, writers expand their sentences by adding unnecessary helping verbs. In the past tense, for example:

Required practices were not *being* followed.

Other writers needlessly turn the present tense into the future:

> Accounts payable *will* determine if the amount is correct and *will* authorize payment.

Passive Voice

Verbs in the passive voice remove action from sentences. Instead of identifying a subject and an action, sentences in the passive voice show a subject being acted upon, receiving an action performed by someone else.

Passive sentences:

The invoices were approved.

The. accounts were not reconciled.

A review was completed.

When sentences are written in the passive voice, readers may not know who performed the action because the writer does not identify the subject. In the examples above, we do not know who approved the invoice, did not reconcile the accounts, or completed the review. The passive voice causes ambiguity. Rewriting the sentences into the active voice requires a subject.

Active sentences:

The supervisor approved the invoices.

The department did not reconcile the accounts.

We completed a review.

To provide a subject in the passive voice, the writer must add a prepositional phrase: The invoices were approved by the supervisor.This is more wordy than the active sentence.

Weaknesses caused by overuse of the passive voice are ambiguity and wordiness. Dull, drawn-out reports typically show a high percentage of sentences in the passive voice. Wordy reports may have between 50 and 75 percent of their sentences in the passive voice. A crisper report uses passive verbs only when necessary, usually 25 to 40 percent of the time.

The preference in concise writing is the active voice, clearly identifying a subject and an action. There are two cases, where passive verbs may be more effective. The first is a situation requiring a softer, more indirect tone. Especially when describing a problem, a direct statement of the subject may be too personal or accusatory. In a small operation, for instance, it may sound like a finger pointing to say, "The clerk did not reconcile the accounts." Therefore, you may choose the more subtle approach of "The accounts were not reconciled." In other cases, responsibility is not clearly defined. You may not be able to identify a unit or person as the subject. If procedures do not exist, or an issue is widespread, you may want to describe the situation in more general terms, such as "Documentation files are not reviewed regularly." This suggests that no review procedure exists, not that an assigned individual is not performing expected duties.

Another danger of passive verbs is their lack of clarity. In recommendations, a passive verb may leave the exact result unclear. For instance: "Complete documentation should be obtained for all new customers."

Such ambiguous wording may allow readers to shift responsibility to undefined "other parties." Yes, documentation should be obtained, but who should do it? A more precise action statement is:"Account officers should completely document new customer information."

Notice the ambiguity in this procedural description:

> A variance analysis is performed for each affiliate. The early transactions ledger and the cash ledger are referenced to determine why there is a **variance**. The balance sheet variances are then explained by analyzing the components of that particular account.

Specifying the subject clarifies responsibility and the sequence of events:

> A staff accountant performs a variance analysis for each affiliate. He refers to the early transactions and cash ledgers to determine the cause of the variance, and analyzes the components of the account to explain the balance-sheet variance.

In the following examples, you will see how wordy passive sentences become.

168

Passive: It is recommended that an updated cost study of floor space be performed. This updated study should be retained by Revenue Planning at least until additional studies are performed in the future. Such studies should be performed on a periodic basis.

Active: Revenue Planning should periodically update the cost study of floor space.

Passive: A procedure has been initiated that requires a receipt to be prepared when such deposits are transferred.

Active: Clerks prepare a receipt when transferring deposits.

Passive: The worksheet is returned to the payroll clerk after it is approved by the Assistant Controller. Once returned, the document is then forwarded to the courier for processing.

Active: The Assistant Controller approves the worksheet and returns it to the payroll clerk, who forwards it to the courier for processing.

Repetition

Sentences may be reduced to as much as half their length by eliminating needless repetition. Here is an illustration:

Forty-one projects, totaling $3,500,000, were examined for proper inclusion in the Capital Budget Report. One project for $43,000 was improperly included in the report because it was not a capital expenditure. One project for $35,000 was improperly included in the report because the approval process was not complete. One project for $500,000 was not properly included in the Capital Budget Report by Corporate Purchasing and was not subsequently caught by the respective division.

Circling the repeated phrases shows how much repetition occurs:

Forty-one projects, totaling $3,500,000, were examined for proper inclusion in the Capital Budget Report. One project for $43,000 was improperly included in the report because it was not a capital expenditure. One project for $35,000 was improperly included in the report because the approval process was not complete. One project for $500,000 was not properly included in the Capital Budget Report by Corporate Purchasing and was not subsequently caught by the respective division.

A concise revision, eliminating the redundancy, follows.

Two projects listed in the Capital Budget Report should not have been included. One, for $43,000, was not a capital expense, and another, for $35,000, was not completed. Another item, totaling $500,000, should have been included in the report but was not.

Here is another paragraph that can be slimmed down to about half its original length:

Payment of invoices is not made within the 15-day period required. Internal Audit's test of 57 invoices paid revealed 53 invoices that were not paid within the 15 days. The average number of days between invoice date and payment date in the sample selected was 40 days.

Revision:
Ninety-three percent of the invoices we tested were paid in an average of 40 days, as compared to the required 15.

Repetition often occurs when items are listed in a series. Identify the repeated phrase, state it once at the beginning of the list, and avoid mentioning it again. To illustrate, consider this list of audit procedures:

The significant audit procedures performed during this examination included:

- Review of the existing system of controls and operating procedures.

- Tests of compliance with Policies and Procedures manual.

- Test of compliance with regulations.
- Review of controls over the quarterly reporting process.
- Review of controls over the compilation and preparation of regulatory reports.

Revision:

We reviewed the following items:

- The unit's system of controls and operating procedures.
- Compliance with Policies and Procedures manual.
- Compliance with regulations.
- Quarterly reporting process.
- Preparation of regulatory reports.

When the list presents similar information for each item, you can present it in a table.

Original Version:

- 46% of the reports tested were not properly completed.
- 5% of the reports tested were not clerically accurate.
- 6% of the reports tested were not signed by the preparer.
- 18% of the reports tested were not approved.

Revision:

Type of Exception	% of Sample
Not properly completed	46%
Inaccurate	5%
Not signed	6%
Unapproved	18%

Extra Articles and Prepositions

Small words can take up a lot of space. Articles and prepositions are often unneeded, and removing them can greatly tighten a sentence. For example:

> The following duties of the accounts payable clerk and the payroll clerk are not adequately segregated, as each performs the following: prepares the manual checks; signs and mails the manual checks.
>
> *Revision:* The accounts payable clerk and payroll clerk both prepare, sign, and mail manual checks.
>
> ---
>
> The report generated through this process is the Combined Register.
>
> *Revision:* This process generates the Combined Register.

Careful attention and discipline in choosing words will make your writing more succinct, focused, and clear. By making yourself aware of common causes of wordiness, you can omit extra words. Even though you may compose your first draft with "too many words," reviewing and editing your narrative will help you prune each sentence and paragraph to just the right size. Remember that shorter is not better in and of itself. Omitting words can change the writer's meaning. As you compose and edit, look for the expression that is both the most succinct and the clearest in conveying your thought.

Avoid filler phrases, statements of the obvious, and references to the writer. Tighten your modifiers, using them only when they add to clarity. Eliminate redundancies. Use the active voice and build sentences around verbs expressed in one or two words. Give every word a purpose, and your writing will be concise.

EDITING AND REVIEWING

12

Editing the
Audit Report

When I ask participants in my writing workshops what they consider to be the number-one writing problem they need to resolve, the topic of editing always appears on the list. Someone—sometimes sheepishly, sometimes aggressively, says, "I want less editing, fewer rewrites. We take too much time in my department to get a report out. It goes through one revision after another, until we don't recognize the original version." This may be a staff member talking, frustrated at the editing done to his or her work, or it may be a manager, dissatisfied with the report drafts submitted by the auditors and with spending too much time being an editor, not a manager. It seems that most audit departments share this problem, but may not recognize its universality. We all seem to have this unspoken and sometimes unrecognized addiction to editing—picking up a pen immediately when asked to review someone else's writing—while we abhor it in others—recoiling at the first sign of red ink we see on our written product.

As with other addictions, no one claims responsibility. Managers say they do not want or like to edit, that they would prefer to do none at all, but that the quality of their staff's writing is not good enough to go to senior management.

Staff members complain that the editing is not necessary at all. Their report is clear and readable; their manager is simply imposing his or her style. The auditor, too, relinquishes responsibility, saying, "Why should I write better? It's going to be changed, anyway."

The Dilemma: To Edit or Not to Edit?

Managers face this decision every day. They review a report, reacting positively to some parts and feeling uncomfortable with others. An item may not be clear or may and need to be stated differently so that readers will understand. A phrase may not sound just right. What does the manager do? He or she can make the changes, let the draft go as it is, or suggest a revision to the writer. The manager makes this decision, considering these questions:

How important is this change?

What's the quickest way of getting this change made?

Who is likely to do the best revision—myself or the writer?

Will the writer be receptive to my suggestion, or will it create less conflict if I just put the change through?

Does this have to be reprinted, anyway, so one more change won't matter?

Almost unconsciously, these thoughts go through the reviewer's mind and the manager makes the editorial decisions.

For writers and editors to resolve the "editing problem," as they so frustratingly label it, they must understand these decision points, act consciously and deliberately in making and receiving editorial changes, and communicate openly about the elements of the editing process.

Reviewing Others' Work

The following techniques will help you be a more constructive and effective reviewer of others' writing:

- Know and apply the appropriate levels of editing.

- Build the writer's pride of authorship.

- Talk to the writer.

- Know your own style.

- **Help manage your team's writing time.**
- **Share responsibility for effective writing.**

To illustrate these points, let's begin with an example of report editing.

A TYPICAL REVIEW

An audit manager receives the following comment from a staff member.

Credit Card Applications

We noted that the record number of applications processed in March 19xx, caused delays in average processing time. The time required to enter applications and follow-up on manual credit bureaus and verifications was strained due to the large volume of applications. As management plans toward increasing the portfolio are fulfilled, application volumes will remain at the current levels. The Credit Card Center must review control and procedures to ensure compliance with Regulation B and to maintain the current applicant satisfaction levels.

Here are the manager's editorial comments:

Credit Card Applications

unnecessary—repeats sentence above

~~We noted that~~ the record number of applications processed in March 19xx, caused delays in average processing time. The time required to enter applications and follow-up on manual credit bureaus and verifications was strained due to the large volume of applications. As ~~management~~ plans ~~toward~~ to increasing the portfolio are completed ~~fulfilled~~, application volumes will remain at the current levels. The Credit Card Center should ~~must~~ review control and procedures to ensure compliance with Regulation B and to maintain the current ~~applicant satisfaction levels~~.

satisfactory processing time.

Know and Apply the Appropriate Levels of Editing

The reviewer's changes illustrate the levels of editing managers typically apply to business documents. Managers may edit at some or all of these four levels:

- Substance
- Readability
- Correctness
- Style

Substance. The first thing most managers look for is the substance of a document. Is the message correct, appropriate, supported, and convincingly presented? The tone and emphasis of the message are part of substance, since they influence the persuasiveness of the writing. The manager's suggestion to quantify the increase in applications and delay in processing time is an example of editing for substance. Another reviewer might revise the opening sentence of this comment to read: "The Credit Card Center is not in compliance with Regulation B. Recent delays in processing time have resulted from a 20% increase in applications." This is an even more substantial change, revising not only the content but the key message. The emphasis now is on compliance, rather than on the growth in applications and processing time.

Readability. Clarity, conciseness, and variety are elements of readability. As reviewers read, they hear the sound of the writing and may suggest or make changes to improve the flow. In the credit card example, the manager eliminated a few phrases and a sentence to make the narrative more concise. The editor also revised an ambiguous phrase, "applicant satisfaction levels," to a simpler, more concrete description, "satisfactory processing time."

Correctness. Correct grammar, and punctuation are important aspects of writing, and every final report must be reviewed for these. The manager has made two punctuation changes in this narrative.

Style. Personal stylistic preferences enter into many managers' editing. Stylistic changes do not alter the meaning, emphasis, tone, or correctness of a narrative. They simply make the reviewer, or the signer, of a document more comfortable. "This sounds more like me," is a comment a reviewer is likely to make to explain a stylistic change. In our example, the manager has changed the word "fulfilled" to "completed," illustrating his own stylistic preference.

A key to managing the editing process effectively is understanding these levels of review and recognizing them in your own editing. Successful editors deliberately decide the levels at which they edit and the manner in which they communicate with writers. Your own success in supporting writers, improving the quality of your department's reports, and managing their timeliness depends on how well you handle the last phase of writing the final editing.

As in any other aspect of managing, there is not one style of editing that will work best in every situation. Variable factors influence the amount and style of your editing. A manager in one company may edit differently than her colleagues at another firm, yet be equally effective. At the same time, managers may work with each of their staff members in different ways to edit the final report.

Variables influencing your levels and style of editing include:

- the number of reviewers of the report,
- time available,
- experience and skills of the writer,
- significance of the desired change, and
- degree of flexibility acceptable.

Your response to these variables will affect how well you accomplish each of the following goals of successful editing.

Build the Writer's Pride of Authorship

Although not all auditors like to write, they all like to have their writing recognized. Unfortunately, some have been discouraged to the point that they no longer expect recognition. They just want to have their writing left intact enough so that they recognize it when they see it in the final report.

Writers have a natural sense of ownership and pride of authorship. Written communication is more personal, more of a self-expression than other methods of presentation or other kinds of work. The auditor who easily accepts a suggestion on the substance of testing or seeks help when making oral presentations may resist editorial changes made to his or her writing. Professional adults know the mechanics of writing, they believe in their own style of expression, and they hold onto their own written words. They do not take editing gently. Believing that writing is their unique personal expression, professionals develop blind spots. Their writing seems to be clear and concise to them, and they feel it exhibits the best choice of content and expression. Pity the reviewer who suggests that it may not.

If you are that editor, you will gain a significant advantage by recognizing and responding to the psychological makeup of your writers. Capitalize on your staff's pride of authorship, and support it to help them strengthen their writing and contribute to the audit team's product. If you destroy their natural pride, you may never be able to rebuild it. If you support and encourage it however, you will be firmly positioned to develop an effective writing team.

When the sense of writers' ownership and pride is cultivated, you will see auditors who are motivated to do their best writing, to learn from editorial feedback, and to share their writing with their colleagues. When writers' pride is damaged, they may give up. They may dislike writing, procrastinate, miss deadlines, and turn in their "first rough draft." Why should they do any more work, they reason, when it's not their report, anyway.

How to Destroy Pride of Authorship

1. *Give inexperienced writers free rein to write as they please, then rewrite to your liking.*

Managers generally have preferred formats, styles, and organizational patterns for their department's reports. Some even have requirements in these areas. The wise manager communicates these expectations to new writers to let them know the boundaries within which they are working. They do not leave new staff members to write as they please, hoping that they will automatically or magically intuit their guidelines.

In their desire to be flexible and accommodating, managers sometimes tell new auditors to write their first report draft on their own, with no guidance, to see what they come up with. The expectation, or hope, is always that this auditor will prove

180

to be a Churchill. The message will be clear, the words will flow beautifully, and the report will need no editing. When the draft appears on the manager's desk, however, the manager's faith begins to slip. The draft is too long, and ideas are unclear. He or she begins editing.

This cycle is well intentioned, but frustrating to new writers. Audit report writing is different from academic writing, research writing, and memo writing. New auditors need to know the general expectations for the audit report—how much detail to include, how to organize comments, what style is acceptable. They need to know that their writing will be reviewed and, probably, edited. An enthusiastic but unconditioned writer may be devastated by having his or her report "rewritten" and may perceive the editing as a reflection on his or her overall performance.

2. *Give only negative feedback.*

Editors keep their pens in hand to make changes or raise questions, not to compliment good writing. Writers are conditioned to look immediately at the number of remarks their boss has made on their report draft, assuming that these are all the things they did wrong. After a while, writers lose sight of their writing strengths and do not notice the bulk of their writing that remains in the final report. They see only the criticism.

Many writers perceive editing as entirely negative and lose perspective on the significance of changes made or suggested. One auditor said that his boss totally changed his reports, that nothing of his style or ideas remained in the final version. When his boss's comments were reviewed, however, it became evident that most of the auditor's original writing was left intact, with some additions made and a few recommendations restated. The auditor had become so accustomed to receiving only changes to his writing, never reinforcement of what he had done well, that he gave up on his writing and lost respect for his own writing skills.

3. *Rewrite.*

For most managers, it is quicker to rewrite a sentence than to discuss it with the writer. This rewrite may be to alter style, or it may change the meaning or emphasis of the sentence. Changing the meaning is the danger of rewriting. The editor may unintentionally alter the message, stating a conclusion that the auditor did not draw from his or her work. When the rewrite is stylistic, writers may perceive the change as unnecessary and as one more indication that their writing is no longer theirs.

4. *Do not discuss your changes with the writer.*

Auditors tell stories of their reports being edited, reprinted, and issued without their having the chance to review the changes. In the worst scenario, the message has changed from the original draft, and the auditor was not consulted on the accuracy of the revised idea. In other cases, the auditor sees a report that smacks of someone else's style. "I didn't write that report," is the usual response to this final, revised version. "That's my boss's report, not mine." The loss of ownership increases.

5. *Impose your style.*

If you have favorite phrases, insist that they appear in all reports. If you don't see them, add them. Change phrases so that your favorite words are included. Reword sentences to make them sound more like the way you would have written them.

Stylistic editing can get out of hand. Writers overreact to differences between their personal style and their boss's. When the boss changes "fulfilled" to "completed," the writer takes it as a personal affront. The more stylistic editing done, the more defensive the writer becomes. Most auditors do not recognize the need to understand and sometimes accept the boss's style, and most bosses do not recognize the need to communicate their stylistic preferences to their staff. As a result, a style war breaks out, with each party supporting his or her favorite phrases.

6. *Let report drafts sit in your in-box.*

After you emphasize the importance of a timely, quality report to management, do you leave report drafts in your in-box for a few days before you get to them?

If you are serious about the value of good writing skills and high-quality reports, communicate their priority by giving prompt feedback on your staff's writing.

Talk to the Writer

The paradox of editing is that the best editing may be done orally. What we think of as a solitary endeavor, righting grammatical wrongs and correcting flow, is in fact a team effort. Some changes can be made quickly and in writing. Others require discussion and joint decision-making.

The goals of communication between editor and writer are to reinforce standards and expectations of effective writing, explain variables influencing style and strategy, and strengthen the writer's skills. Communication must take place before and during the editing.

What Managers Can Communicate Before the Report Is Written. In an established audit team, expectations for content, organization, format, and style may be understood by all members, and little communication may be required before the staff writes the report draft.

Writers may need instructions or guidance only in unusual circumstances, when the tone or level of detail will be significantly different from the typical report.

In a newer group, where the members have not worked together before as a writing team, with a new auditor, or when reporting format or style is changing, early communication can save time and reduce frustration in both writing and editing. In these cases, the reviewer may communicate:

- criteria for report writing,

- due dates for first draft and final report, and

- editorial style.

Criteria for Report Writing. Some general instructions build consistency in your department's style and save time for all writers. The report organization, labeling of sections, and stylistic conventions should be standard and known by all writers. Criteria for clarity, conciseness, and directness should be stated concretely. Although no writer or editor can expect or use a formulaic list, guidelines can greatly aid communication and consistency. This book has offered quality checklists, summary outlines, and sample worksheets that you may adapt as your standards. Share them with your writers. Get their suggestions and incorporate them.

Standards and guidelines are more effective than detailed instructions and style books. Too much detail about report expectations can stifle creativity or lead to a boring sameness of style and flow in all your reports. Using samples of past reports may be useful to give new auditors an overview of the department's writing, but this should be done sparingly. Once a manager labels a report as a good one, inexperienced writers tend to copy more than its structure; they also copy language, tone, and habits. The result again is predictability in report writing.

Recognize and communicate to writers that variable factors will influence the tone, word choice, and organizational strategies used in a report. These situational factors must be appropriate to each audit and cannot be defined for all reports. Be sure writers understand why these elements may vary. In unusual situations, talk to the writer after the closing meeting but before report writing to agree on the variables.

Due dates. Be sure your team knows the standards for timeliness. Help writers plan their writing time by indicating the date you expect the report draft and the day the final report will be issued. To control timeliness, hold writers to their due dates. Put timeliness standards at the top of your quality control lists. Measure individual and overall timeliness of reports.

Editing style. Let your writers know what you will be looking for by talking about your expectations or sharing written standards. Tell

184

them how you prefer to review a report—discussing items with them in a meeting, or making comments on the report for them to review. Decide the level at which you will edit, and communicate that, too.

How Managers Can Communicate During the Editing Process. Your role as an editor is to coach writers, offering concrete and constructive guidance. Remarks such as "unclear," "too long," or "good" do not offer much direction to the writer. Your feedback should consist of a specific question or suggestion for change and your reason. For example, in the credit card comment, the reviewer may: "What is the specific growth in volume? How many days does it take to process applications? Tell the reader exactly how big the problem is." The comment asks for specific information and provides the rationale. In marking the second sentence as "Unnecessary. Repeats sentence above," the editor makes a suggestion for improving readability, listing the cause in the margin. Other examples of concrete, constructive feedback are: "Good balance of positive and negative." "Right amount of detail." "Passive voice." "Phrase is drawn-out."

For more major issues of substance, such as lack of clarity, the reviewer may need to talk through the item with the writer. Asking the right questions and taking notes may help build an outline in the auditor's own words. With that discussion and framework, the writer can go back to work, filling in the outline using his or her own words, secure in the overall structure and clarity.

Concrete guidance does not have to be blunt or insensitive criticism. Present your comments tactfully. With a less experienced or struggling writer, have a face-to-face meeting to discuss your questions and feedback. Work through the issues together, allowing the auditor to participate as much as possible. Don't mandate, but collaborate on decisions. Be responsive to the writer's good suggestions and accepting of reasonable explanations. For a very sensitive writer, keep your notes and questions on a separate page or in the margin to avoid the look of a "red-inked" document.

It may seem that all this conversation will take a lot of time and effort on the part of the manager. The first time you review a report this way, it will. The more you work with the same writer, however, the more response you will see to your coaching and the less review time you will need to spend. Also, as you get to know each other's styles, you will not have to talk through every change or suggestion. A simple note in the margin, such as "wordy," "ambiguous," or "jargon," may be fully understood and accepted by a writer who knows your expectations. Your queries in the margin may stand on their own, also.

In the short-term, coaching will take more time. In the long-term, you will establish more effective communication among your team and build stronger writing skills among your staff.

Know Your Own Style

Your personal style will inevitably influence your editing. If you are aware of your own preferences and know when you are making stylistic changes, you can manage this part of your editing and decide when it is appropriate. This judicial application of your editing privilege will build greater receptivity among your staff.

If you are editing a report or other document you will sign, stylistic editing is your prerogative. You will want the writing to sound like yours, with words and phrasing you are comfortable with. If your name will not appear on the document, you have less reason to apply your own style. In those circumstances, writers may be responsive to your suggestions for substantive changes, but may not welcome changes in expression.

When you do edit for style, be tactful. Recognize and acknowledge stylistic differences between you and your staff. The examples, worksheets, and discussions in this book have helped you identify your own writing style. Use them as a basis for discussion with your staff. Talk about differences in the way you write. Let them know of expressions you particularly dislike or especially prefer. Stylistic editing should not be a major issue in the review process, and will not be as long as you label it for what it is and do not force your style on your staff's permanent writing habits.

The potential danger in openly discussing style is that you may be afraid of sounding too commanding. You will sound this way if you present your stylistic requests in the tone of "I want it said this way," or "We're changing it because I like it better the other way." Use softer language, such as "This word sounds more like me," or "Your word is fine, but I wouldn't use it." To reinforce your image as a reasonable editor, never say "never." Some audit directors tire of overused phrases and forbid them in their department's reports. Some audit directors have banned the words "however," "which," "not," and "should." They did so for good reason—their staffs were overusing them—but their mandates of "never" caused resentment.

Where possible, avoid editing simply because of your stylistic preference. Counter writers' perceptions that editing is purely for style. Concentrate on the substance, tone, readability, and correctness. Allow enough flexibility for writers to express themselves in their own words and develop their own style. Allow them to continue building their pride of authorship.

Help Manage Your Team's Writing Time

Coach your staff to develop efficient writing habits by composing along the way. Encourage them to use summaries, outlines, and audit comment worksheets and to write these throughout the audit, as they complete sections of work. Work with them to set deadlines, and stick to those deadlines. Good habits of composition can help develop more efficient writers.

For a team project, though, the writing is not finished when the deadline is reached and the first draft is put together. Review steps are part of the process and must be handled just as well as the writing if the team is to make its final deadline of issuing the report. As a team leader, here are some things you can do to help keep the process on track.

1. *Decide on editing responsibilities.*

If more than one person is reviewing the report draft, separate the levels of editing to minimize overlap that may lead to extensive revising. If four people review the report, and each one edits for his or her own style, you will end up with four revisions of the report and no one completely satisfied with the final product. Especially when editing for style, limit the review to one person. If the highest-level manager likes to see his or her style reflected in the report, let that person do the stylistic editing and discipline yourself and the other reviewers to skip this editorial step. Similarly, one reviewer may be stronger than others in grammar and language and may take on the role of editing for grammar.

Generally, the first level of supervisory review concentrates on the substance of the report and higher levels should have to raise fewer questions on content.

2. *Review along the way.*

If writers are summarizing or outlining their major points throughout the audit, you can help keep the process moving by reviewing

187

these as they are done. If a writer composes a full draft and your editing concentrates significantly on the substance, you have lost all the time the writer spent polishing readability, flow, and correctness. For large audits or when working with less skilled writers, agree on the substance and organization of comments before the complete narrative is written. Use the audit comment worksheet, or another outline, to review the logic and completeness of the issues. If the audit team is large, a group meeting may be efficient to present all possible items for the report, consolidate them, agree on the outline, and assign the writing. After the closing meeting with line management, recap the results with the audit team to be sure that writers are clear on any revisions needed to the content or tone of the draft report.

3. *Use peer review.*

An objective reader can provide invaluable feedback on the clarity and completeness of a narrative. Encourage team members to share their drafts with each other or with another member of the department not involved in the audit. This will improve clarity and catch major weaknesses or omissions before the writer submits his or her writing for managerial review.

4. *Monitor timeliness of reporting.*

Show that you take the timeliness of reports seriously by enforcing deadlines, editing report drafts promptly, and tracking timeliness throughout other phases of the writing and editing process. Encourage reports to move along swiftly by attaching a routing slip to all reviewers, requiring initials and date of review. Encourage efficient editing and writing habits in your department.

Share Responsibility for Effective Writing

Even with the best editorial skills and coaching abilities, a manager can neither take on complete responsibility for the quality of reports nor expect dramatic and immediate changes in the staff's writing skills. Responsibility for quality must lie with the writers, and so managers may need to provide training and references to auditors to help them improve their skills. Feedback alone may not be enough. If staffs do not have the ability or the resources to correct identified writing weaknesses, editorial feedback may be frustrating. This may happen with the well-intentioned use of the automated style now available for word processors. Auditors may learn from this package that their writing style is passive, but may not know enough about the voices of verbs to be able to change this.

A productive approach to helping writers strengthen their skills includes these steps:

- Work with the individual to identify writing strengths and areas of development.

   Have the writer do a self-assessment first.

   Use objective criteria and specific examples.

- Develop a plan of action, outlining priority goals and resources to be used.

- Provide resources: training, reference books, examples, coaching.

- Evaluate progress.

- Direct feedback to the individual's goals when editing report drafts.

- Schedule periodic reviews of progress.

A training class provided in a vacuum will be of limited value. The writer may not perceive his or her weaknesses and so have little motivation to learn or the writer may not be able to use the new skills on the job, because the boss's stylistic expectations are so different from those presented in the training. When you provide training, do so within the context of the plan outlined above. Discuss goals before the workshop, and expect feedback from the writer on his or her return. After the seminar, set specific writing goals and measure results.

Remember that individuals improve their writing skills at different speeds. Be responsive to the person's unique skills and learning style. The following chart offers guidelines on methods for overcoming different areas of writing weaknesses.

Writing Weakness	How to overcome
Substance	Discuss expectations. Define report

	standards. Give training geared to internal audit report writing.
Readability	Give training in audit or business writing skills. Provide exercises and coaching. Give ongoing feedback.
Style	Discuss individual and departmental expectations for style. Highlight examples of preferred and disliked styles.
Correctness	Use grammar reference books. Consider refresher courses or self-study. Explain rationale behind grammatical corrections.

Editing Your Own Work

No one writes a perfect first draft. Before you issue a report or any other kind of writing, or before you turn a draft in for review, edit your writing for clarity, conciseness, and readability. Be sure you are presenting your best work to your recipient or reviewer. If you are editing your own work, take these steps:

- Write the first draft, concentrating on substance: message, support, emphasis, and tone.
- Let the draft cool, preferably overnight.
- Use review checklists, such as those in this book, to edit.
- Read first for overall meaning: logic, flow, and completeness.
- Edit for readability and correctness.
- Make changes to the document and print it.
- Proofread.
- Run spelling verifier.

190

Editing Tools

Exhibits 12-1, 12-2 provide tools editors will find useful in making editing more objective and efficient. These include "Guidelines for Editing Audit Comments and the Audit Report," and "References."

Choosing your editorial style deliberately and giving balanced feedback to writers will make your editing process smoother, faster, and more constructive. Remember the following variables.

Variable	High	Low
Number of reviewers	Limit your level of edit.	Assign an editor to cover all levels.
Time	Discuss required revisions.	May need to make more suggestions and changes, have less talk.
Writers' skills	Allow independent revisions.	Coach. Provide training.
Significance	Make a direct change.	Suggest an alternative. Be flexible.
Flexibility	Avoid editing.	Explain rationale for change.

Whatever the situation and whatever approach to editing you are using, you can make it a positive experience for writer and reviewer alike. If you can build the writers' pride of authorship, encourage open communication, help manage your group's writing time, and share responsibility for good writing, you will see improved report drafts, develop better writers among your staff, and reduce your own time spent editing.

EXHIBIT 12-1

Guidelines for Editing Audit Comments

1. Read for overall meaning.

2. Review for substance: content and tone.

3. Discuss substantial changes with the writer.

4. Edit for conciseness, concreteness, and clarity.

Guidelines for Editing the Audit Report

1. Organize all audit comments.

    Look for common themes.

    Consolidate items.

    Do a final edit for tone and content.

    Determine the overall conclusion or opinion.

2. Arrange final comments in order of importance.

3. Edit for consistency:

    Style of headings

    Proper use of numbers

    Consistency of titles, abbreviations, etc.

    Definition of terms and acronyms

    Parallelism of items in a series

4. Edit for conciseness, concreteness, and clarity.

5. Write the executive summary.

6. Check for consistency of order and wording between the executive summary and the body.

7. Add cover sheet, table of contents, etc.

EXHIBIT 12-2

References

To check rules of grammar and language use, use a good reference book. The following books are complete and easy-to-use guides.

Brusaw, Charles T.; Alred, Gerald J.; and Oliu, Walter E. *The Business Writer's Handbook,* Second edition. New York: St. Martin's Press, 1982.

Cook, Claire Kehrwald. *The MLA'S Line by Line: How to Edit Your Own Writing.* Boston: Houghton Mifflin Company, 1985.

Fowler, H. Ramsey. *The Little, Brown Handbook,* Third edition. Boston: Little, Brown and Company, 1986.

About the Author

Angela J. Maniak is an independent consultant specializing in communication skills for internal auditors. She has consulted to audit departments in all industries to help them increase the effectiveness of their communication with executive management.

Ms. Maniak has held positions as Director of Audit Professional Practices for Bank of Boston, Program Manager for Audit Education at Bank Administration Institute, and Technical Editor for the Federal Reserve Bank of Chicago.

Her publications include *Presenting Results, Writing Effective Audit Reports,* and *Clear Writing: Rx for Foggy Audit Reports.* She is a recipient of the Institute of Internal Auditors' John B. Thurston Award for outstanding publication.

Ms. Maniak, whose B.A. and M.A. are from Indiana University, is a frequent speaker for many professional auditing associations.

About the Publisher

PROBUS PUBLISHING COMPANY

Probus Publishing Company fills the informational needs of today's business professional by publishing authoritative, quality books on timely and relevant topics, including:

- Investing
- Futures/Options Trading
- Banking
- Finance
- Marketing and Sales
- Manufacturing and Project Management
- Personal Finance, Real Estate, Insurance and Estate Planning
- Entrepreneurship
- Management

Probus books are available at quantity discounts when purchased for business, educational or sales promotional use. For more information, please call the Director, Corporate/Institutional Sales at 1-800-PROBUS-1, or write:

Director, Corporate/Institutional Sales
Probus Publishing Company
1925 N. Clybourn Avenue
Chicago, Illinois 60614
FAX (312) 868-6250